The
Living Trust
Simplified

STEPHEN C. BRECHT

HASTINGS HOUSE
Book Publishers
141 HALSTEAD AVENUE, MAMARONECK, N.Y. 10543

Library of Congress Catalog Card Number 93-080523

. ISBN 0-8038-9361-2

Text design by Irving Perkins Associates
Cover design © by One+One Studio

Distributed by Publishers Group West
Emeryville, California

Printed in the United States of America
10 9 8 7 6 5 4 3 2 1

Acknowledgments

I want to thank my publisher, Hy Steirman, for all his help and assistance in the shaping of this book. His insights and experience freed the figure from the stone. It is a better work because of his contribution.

I also want to thank my estate planning associate. Theron Murphy. Without his encouragement, help, and support, this book might never have been written.

Contents

The Living Trust Simplified contains material that is intended to explain the mechanics, use, and benefits of the revocable living trust, and is designed to provide information to help the reader find and work with a qualified estate planning professional. It is neither a substitute for, nor an attempt to provide, legal advice. The author, publisher, their agents and assignees are not engaged in rendering legal, accounting, or other professional services or advice.

Though every attempt has been made to provide current and up-to-date information, it should be checked with a professional against the most recent changes and developments in federal and state laws. The author, publisher, their agents and assignees cannot be held accountable for any error or omission contained herein, nor in any other associated materials.

—STEPHEN C. BRECHT

The
Living Trust
Simplified

What Is a Living Trust?

A living trust is a document created during one's lifetime whereby that person sets up the mechanism to retain full control of his/her assets and, upon passing, to transfer those assets legally to the chosen heirs quickly and privately without court intrusion. It usually is revocable, meaning that during his/her lifetime, that person may alter any of its terms and even cancel the trust completely.

An irrevocable living trust is just that: irrevocable. The terms and conditions of this type of trust cannot be modified or revoked except, under certain conditions, by court order.

The great benefits of trusts are that they avoid costly probate court costs and lawyers' fees, as well as save on taxes and maintain family control over the management of your estate and its distribution to your heirs. And it's all legal.

Putting It All Together

When you consider creating a living trust, you should think of using it to accomplish a specific goal or set of goals. The most important of those goals is the financial management of your estate. Sound financial planning consists of several parts, like pieces of a jigsaw puzzle that fit together to form a complete and comprehensive picture. This planning puzzle consists of the following pieces:

Retirement planning. We all want to spend our retirement years with as much financial security as possible, but a financially sound retirement doesn't just happen. You have to plan for it years in advance. If you don't, your "golden years" may turn out to be less than happy ones.

Investment planning. This centers around the acquiring and management of investments for your benefit. Which stocks and bonds to buy or sell? Should real estate be a part of your asset package? Are gold and other precious metals smart buys? What level of safety do you need in an investment? What about return "on" your investments? What about return "of" your investments? By making the right choices, you may increase the size of your estate by thousands of dollars over your lifetime.

Tax planning. All of us are obliged to pay taxes. Yet, we should not be expected to pay more taxes than we are obligated to pay. Proper tax planning can save you thousands of dollars during your lifetime.

Protection planning. This concerns the financial protection of your family due to loss of income if you become incapacitated, or if you pass away, while at the same time protects your estate from being liquidated to pay estate taxes. All of these planning areas are extremely important and proper attention should be paid to them. It is recommended that they be carefully investigated in order for your family to receive maximum benefit from your estate.

2

This book addresses *estate planning*. Of all areas of financial planning, it's the one that would result in your family's receiving the most return per dollar spent. It is the centerpiece of effective planning and management.

Cornerstone of Planning

When you enter into estate planning and are working on a living trust, you might also consider a "revocable" living trust. This is the setting up of a living trust with yourself as grantor and trustee. If some years from now you change your mind, or your family or financial situation changes, then you are legally able to "revoke" the trust, hence the word *revocable*. A properly drawn revocable living trust is the cornerstone of proper estate planning.

There is an old saying in Hollywood that points out, "If the story doesn't make sense, everything else is wasted." The same is true for you. If your estate planning doesn't make sense, or is flawed, then everything you place on top of it—such as your retirement planning, investment planning, tax planning, and protection planning—could very easily be wasted.

Are You Taking It with You?

"You can't take it with you." We have all heard that saying many times before. I knew a man once who, knowing that he couldn't take it with him, decided to send it on ahead. His problem was, he didn't know the address. Whenever I hear the expression "You can't take it with you," I am reminded of an old burlesque joke:

Old Joe was on his deathbed and determined to take his money with him. He was smart enough to know that he couldn't do it by himself, and would need some help. So he called on his three most trusted advisers and friends—his clergyman, his physician, and his lawyer.

At his bedside, Joe told them of his plan. "Dear and trusted friends," he said, "I am departing this earth and have decided to take my estate with me when I go. In order to do this, I have liquidated my assets and I'm giving each of you one hundred thousand dollars in cash with the provision that when I pass away, you will put the money in my coffin. Would you please do this for me, my dear friends?"

"Yes, yes indeed!" came the replies. They all would be happy to help their old friend by honoring his last request.

After several days, the old gentleman passed away. At his funeral, the three friends were discussing his final wish. The lawyer turned to the clergyman and asked, "Reverend, did you put the money in Joe's coffin as he requested?"

The reverend was nervous. He gazed heavenward for

4

a moment, then turned back to the lawyer and said, "To be perfectly honest, no. The church is in a bad state of repair. It needs a new roof. I didn't think Joe would mind if I took ten thousand dollars and donated it to the building fund in his name. The rest of the cash went into his coffin."

The lawyer then turned to the doctor and asked him about his promise to put his share of the cash into Joe's coffin. The doctor, being a man of the world, glared at the lawyer and said, "Look, there are many pressing needs in this world, and medical research is certainly among the most urgent. I knew that Joe couldn't use the money where he was going, so I took fifty thousand dollars and donated it to medical research in his name. The other fifty thousand in cash went into Joe's coffin."

With this, the lawyer turned upon his friends and started to berate them. "How could you do this?" he asked. "You promised him on his deathbed that you would comply with his wishes. I want both of you to know that I put my *personal check* for the full one hundred thousand dollars into his coffin!"

This humorous anecdote does have a moral, IF YOU DON'T DO SOME PROPER ESTATE PLANNING NOW, MUCH OF YOUR HARD-EARNED MONEY WILL END UP IN THE BANK ACCOUNT OF A LAWYER!

So, if you can't take it with you, where does your estate go after you pass away?

What Usually Happens and Why

Most of you have heard of the word *probate*. What does it mean? Why do the courts get involved in your estate after you've passed away?

Let me give you a simple definition. Probate means "to prove." Probate is the process by which your name is removed from a title or an asset and your will "proved" valid, your legal and financial matters are settled, your creditors are paid, and, finally, the remainder of your assets are distributed to your beneficiaries (heirs).

Thus, if you pass away possessing real estate, bank accounts, stocks or bonds as an individual owner, your name will have to be removed from all those assets before they can be transferred. But transferred to whom? You aren't here with us anymore and can no longer sign over those assets to your heirs. All fifty states have established a process whereby the state, through the court, takes over control of your estate to make sure that your affairs are settled and your assets transferred, hopefully in accordance with your wishes. This process is called probate.

If your estate should fall under the jurisdiction of the probate court, that court will have almost full and total control over your estate and all its assets while your affairs are sorted out.

They Said, "Sell It . . . Now!"

The probate court's control over your estate can go so far as to force the sale of assets in your estate in order to pay off a debt. For example, if that asset is real estate, the court could force a sale in a down market. Consequently, that asset would not provide a maximum return and the dollar value of the estate would be decreased substantially. The same would hold true for stocks, bonds, business interests, art, collectibles, and anything else you owned at the time of your passing. If your estate is debt free at the time, then the probate process itself becomes a debt against the estate and your assets can be sold to pay the court and lawyers' fees—*to pay the very people who are forcing the sale of your estate in the first place!*

It Takes a Lifetime, or Two, to Build Your Estate

What exactly is an estate? Simply put, it's *everything* you own. It consists of all your personal property—your automobiles, boats, planes, motor homes, furniture, appliances, art, stamps and coins, your dishes, and even the clothes on your back. It consists of any real estate you might own, including your home, any investment properties, commercial properties, vacant land, even vacation time-shares. It encompasses your cash accounts, such as checking, savings, money market funds, CDs, treasury notes, retirement accounts, annuities, and life insurance policies. Your estate is also made up of any stocks, bonds, mutual funds, secured notes, trust deeds (mortgages), partnerships, outstanding loans, and any business agreements you might have. All of these items make up your "estate."

Estate Planning and You

When you consider estate planning, you actually are referring to two separate processes that are very different from each other. The first process is the acquisition and management of all the assets in your estate for your benefit during your lifetime. This management is centered around making sure that you get the most return out of those assets.

The second part of estate planning concerns how the assets, acquired over your lifetime (and your spouse's), should be distributed after your passing. To build up an estate, the average American will work approximately eighty-six thousand hours during a lifetime. This equals forty years of full-time work. Yet, believe it or not, most people do little, if any, estate planning. They have worked hard for all those years to build up what they have. Yet, surprisingly, these very people do little or nothing to protect their estates for their families. This is especially sad, since proper estate planning is so easy to accomplish.

Estate Planning Challenge
I. GETTING THE RIGHT INFORMATION

There are several challenges in estate planning. The first, and most important, is to find the information you need in order to educate yourself about estate planning options. Ask yourself the following questions:

Whom can I talk to in order to get the information I need to begin my estate planning?

Where can I go to get this information?

I know I must do something, but what? What are my choices?

It is not surprising that most people will turn to a lawyer for answers to these questions. They assume that since most lawyers know about wills and probate, they would also know about living trusts, avoiding probate, and estate planning in general.

Several years ago, a senior citizen consumer advocate group surveyed lawyers about their knowledge of living trusts and estate planning. When the information was tabulated, the results stunned the researchers. It revealed that less than 2 percent of the lawyers knew anything about living trusts or their use in estate planning. It shouldn't be surprising. Like most doctors, lawyers specialize in such areas as divorce, corporate law, marine law, international law, union negotiations, trial work, criminal law, civil law, etc. So it's not surprising for lawyers to tell their clients that all they need is a will. They do this for two reasons:

1. They are not fully informed and, in many cases, have little knowledge about setting up living trusts.
2. It is in the lawyers' self-interest for you to have a will. As it usually requires an attorney to move a will through the probate court, the most likely candidate for this job will be your lawyer—the very lawyer who told you, "All you really need is a will."

Many people are intimidated by lawyers, especially those who've had little or no professional contact with them. In the first place, how do you hire a lawyer? Will the price be fair? Will you be charged by the hour or will it be a set fee? What about the quality of the documents and service?

In addition, many people are concerned that somehow the lawyer may take over control of their estate and assets. This does happen from time to time. Whether lawyers deserve the reputation or not, many people think of them as opportunists. However, there are reliable attorneys who specialize in estate planning, though one does not have to be a lawyer to be a qualified estate planner.

Estate Planning Challenge
II. AVOIDING PROBATE

Another important estate planning challenge is the avoidance of probate. I will define the process further and show you why probate is a tragedy waiting to happen.

A TYPICAL PROBATE

Let's look at the case of the Stephensons, a family consisting of Dad, Mom, and three kids. What will happen to their estate if Mr. and/or Mrs. Stephenson passes away? How will this estate be transferred to the three Stephenson children?

In all probability, little or no estate planning was done, or, perhaps, there might be a will, so the Stephenson estate will fall under the jurisdiction of the probate court. That court will have complete control of the family assets, and the Stephenson children literally will be at the mercy of the court.

Probate Problems
I. TIME

One negative thing about probate is that it is a time-consuming process. Papers are filed and then you wait . . . file more papers, and wait some more . . . file still more papers, and still wait . . . file and wait . . . file and wait! Consequently, the Stephensons' probate can easily take anywhere from a few months to one or two *years*. During this period, the family will not have control of their assets. If it was the father who passed away and all assets were in his name, day-to-day living expenses would have to be requested and approved (or not approved) by the court. Important opportunities could be lost while the estate is locked up in probate court.

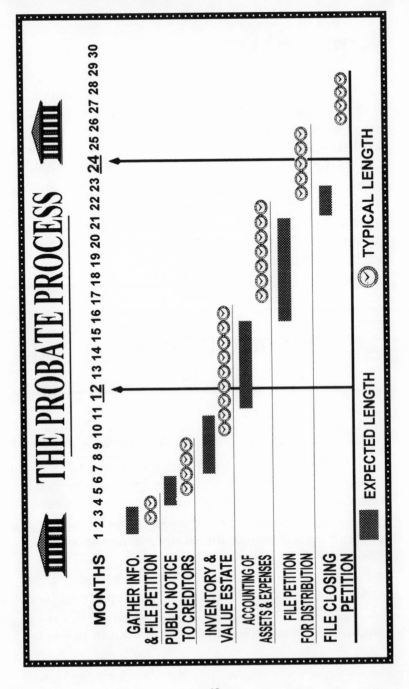

THE PROBATE PROCESS

MONTHS 1 2 3 4 5 6 7 8 9 10 11 12 13 14 15 16 17 18 19 20 21 22 23 24 25 26 27 28 29 30

GATHER INFO.
& FILE PETITION

PUBLIC NOTICE
TO CREDITORS

INVENTORY &
VALUE ESTATE

ACCOUNTING OF
ASSETS & EXPENSES

FILE PETITION
FOR DISTRIBUTION

FILE CLOSING
PETITION

EXPECTED LENGTH   TYPICAL LENGTH

12

In some states, probate may have a shorter statutory time frame, but in many states, this process can often drag on and on for much longer than one or two years. This is because of challenges to the will, or estates that cannot be settled due to other reasons.

Let's look at a challenge to a will. If a will is challenged in the probate court by a disappointed heir (perhaps the child of a previous marriage or a first wife), the probate process comes to a complete halt until the challenge is settled. After this settlement, the probate process will then pick up where it left off and grind forward slowly.

Some lawyers may offer to help a disappointed heir challenge a will on a contingent fee basis, that is, the lawyer will get a percentage of what he/she wins for their client. The lawyer knows the assets remain frozen in probate court and that frequently the other heirs will become frustrated or will be in need of money and in many cases will settle just to end the agony of the probate process. With careful estate planning, all this can be avoided. It is rare for a revocable living trust to be challenged on a contingent fee basis. This is because assets are not locked up in court, but are in the hands of the beneficiaries. A lawyer, hired to challenge a living trust, will want his/her fee up front prior to starting a case. This acts as a deterrent to any challenges to your wishes as stipulated in your living trust.

Probate Problems

II. COST

Another problem with probate is its cost. Probate is incredibly expensive in wasted time, dollars, and emotions.

While the Stephenson estate is under control of the probate court, it is being managed for a fee by an outside attorney appointed by the court. This fee will average somewhere between 4 percent to 11 percent of the *gross value* of the estate, before debts, liens, taxes, etc., are deducted.

Lawyers are allowed to bill the estate for "extraordinary fees" and for "services rendered" over and above the minimum percentage mandated by the state. This is sanctioned by the court, and the heirs have no say in the matter. For example, in many states, probate starts at a minimum 4 percent of the estate. However, when everything is settled, the estate often pays closer to 8 percent of the gross value. Thus, the lawyer's fee amounts to $16,000 on a $200,000 estate. If the heirs hired their own attorney, add those fees deducted from the estate. What if the estate were $600,000? The court-appointed lawyer would be allowed fees of $48,000. These are costs that can be avoided.

Because of a lack of knowledge, extra fees are being charged thousands of times daily all over America. It's a financial burden on heirs that is avoidable with proper estate planning!

Probate Problems
III. PRIVACY

Loss of privacy is another problem activated by the probate process. When the Stephenson estate falls under the jurisdiction of the probate court, it suddenly becomes a matter of public record. Sometimes, parts of a will become subject matter for the media. Anyone and everyone in town can go to the court and ask the clerk to see their file. They will know exactly what the family assets are and who the beneficiaries are.

Indeed, there are unscrupulous salesmen and scam artists who use and abuse these records, uncovering who has come into money recently or who will receive a large inheritance in the near future. They will solicit these people with numerous products and schemes, many of them worthless. Widows with a lot of cash, who often have had little experience in investing, are the favorite targets for these schemers. Consequently, many a widow is broke eighteen months after the death of her husband.

With proper estate planning, this misfortune is avoidable.

Estate Planning Challenge
III. TAXES

Another estate planning challenge concerns the payment of taxes. Upon your passing, the federal, and some state, governments will want their "fair share" of everything you leave behind. On large estates, this "fair share" can be as high as 55 percent of the estate's assets!

FEDERAL ESTATE TAXES

The federal inheritance tax rate starts at the same rate as the federal gift tax. It is a very confiscatory tax structure. Estate and gift taxes are levied in a manner much like that of income taxes. As the value of the estate increases, the tax brackets change and the percentage of tax levied increases.

For example, if you have an estate of $1,000,000, you may conclude you're a millionaire, and that it will all be put to good use for the benefit of your family. But Uncle Sam is going to say, "Wait a minute, Mr. or Mrs. Millionaire. On that taxable million, you have a unified credit of $600,000 [see below]; of the $400,000, you have graduated taxes of 37 percent to 39 percent. Plus, I'll take 41 percent of every dollar between $1,000,000 and $1,250,000," and so on.

THE UNIFIED CREDIT

Each person has a unified credit, which will reduce the amount of estate tax that may have to be paid. It is equivalent to having $600,000 worth of assets not subject to the federal inheritance tax; $1,200,000 for a married couple with proper estate planning.

ESTATE TAX CALCULATOR

The following tax calculator may be used as a general guide for answering two important questions:

1. Will my estate be subject to federal inheritance tax?
2. If this tax has to be paid, how much will it be?

This calculator is based on the assumption that no unified credit has been used by the decedent prior to the individual's passing. It should not be substituted for more detailed accounting procedures.

This calculator does not reflect any state and local taxes that may be levied against your estate.

Please note percentage rates on chart marked with single asterisk. The Budget Reconciliation Act of 1993 lowered the rates from 53 percent to 50 percent, 55 percent to 50 percent, and 60 percent to 55 percent respectively.

In addition, note double asterisk on chart. Estates are subject to a 5 percent surcharge on assets exceeding $10,000,000 until the benefits of the unified credit and the lower graduated tax brackets have been recaptured. In other words, until the entire taxable estate is taxed at a flat 55 percent.

Inheritance Tax Calculator

At Time of Passing of Individual or First Spouse, an Estate Valued at . . . Net Value	Percentage Rate Brackets for Federal Inheritance Tax. Tax Paid	Single Individual Without Using a Trust or Using A Single Living Trust. Tax Paid	Married Couple Without Using a Trust or Using A Married Living Trust. Tax Paid	Married Couple Using an A-B Married Living Trust. Tax Paid
$600,000	37%	$0	$0	$0
$625,000	37%	$9,250	$9,250	$0
$650,000	37%	$18,500	$18,500	$0
$700,000	37%	$37,000	$37,000	$0
$750,000	37%	$55,500	$55,500	$0
$800,000	39%	$75,000	$75,000	$0
$850,000	39%	$94,500	$94,500	$0
$900,000	39%	$114,000	$114,000	$0
$1,000,000	39%	$153,000	$153,000	$0
$1,100,000	41%	$194,000	$194,000	$0
$1,200,000	41%	$235,000	$235,000	$0
$1,300,000	43%	$277,000	$277,000	$42,000
$1,400,000	43%	$320,000	$320,000	$85,000
$1,500,000	43%	$363,000	$363,000	$128,000
$1,600,000	45%	$408,000	$408,000	$173,000
$1,700,000	45%	$453,000	$453,000	$218,000
$1,800,000	45%	$498,000	$498,000	$263,000
$1,900,000	45%	$543,000	$543,000	$308,000
$2,000,000	45%	$588,000	$588,000	$353,000
$3,000,000	50%*	$1,275,000	$1,275,000	$889,000
$5,000,000	50%*	$2,275,000	$2,275,000	$1,889,000
$10,000,000	55%* **	$4,948,000	$4,948,000	$4,713,000

If you have an estate of $3,000,000 at the time of your passing, Uncle Sam is going to take $1,290,800.

Proper estate planning will eliminate headaches and maximize the inheritance for your heirs.

Federal "Tax Breaks"
I. THE UNLIMITED MARITAL DEDUCTION

There are two tax exemptions you should be aware of that are known as "tax breaks."

The first tax exemption is the unlimited marital deduction, which benefits only married couples. It's a simple, easy-to-understand situation. If you're married at the time of your passing, you can simply "gift" *all* of your assets, your entire estate, to your surviving spouse, free of any federal inheritance or gift taxes. There is no limit as to the size of your estate—it can be $1,000,000,000 and there will still be no inheritance taxes levied by Uncle Sam.

The one major problem with married couples using this "tax break" is that when the surviving spouse passes away, the estate could be hit with heavy federal inheritance taxes. In an estate over $3,000,000, this could be as high as 55 percent.

Federal "Tax Breaks"
II. PERSONAL ESTATE EXEMPTION

The other inheritance "tax break" applies to everyone, whether single, married, widowed, or divorced. It's called the personal estate exemption, and you have it automatically: if at the time of your passing, the *net value* of all the assets in your estate is less than $600,000, there will be no federal estate taxes. Keep in mind that Uncle Sam includes everything you own when determining the net value of your estate. This includes property, securities, art, furniture, jewelry, even the face value of your life insurance policies.

But there is a catch that you should be aware of. When you pass away, $600,000 will be exempt from inheritance taxes, and when your spouse passes away, another $600,000 will be exempt. Does that mean you could actually leave $1,200,000 to your kids without taxes?

No! That thinking can cost your estate a small fortune. Unless you prepare your estate properly, you will be able to take advantage of only one $600,000 exemption, because after you die, the tax-free $600,000 the spouse inherited now becomes part of the estate. A warning to married couples. If you elect to "gift" the unlimited marital deduction to your spouse, you will be losing one of your two major exemptions unless you do some estate planning. Why throw away approximately $200,000 that could benefit your family?

Asset Distribution Techniques

What are the current methods available for distributing the estate to your heirs upon your passing?

There are three basic estate distribution techniques.

1. The first and most common method is to do nothing.
2. The second is to use a will. Most people believe that a will provides all the protection needed for their family.
3. The third is to establish a *trust*. The most widely used trust is the revocable living trust.

Here's a review of each of these techniques, and how they function in the distribution of your estate to your loved ones.

Distribution Technique
I. DO NOTHING

What if you *do nothing*? Absolutely nothing at all. This is the technique used by almost 70 percent of all Americans to distribute their estates. People use this technique for several reasons:

1. They feel immortal. There will no need to distribute their estates. That may sound foolish, but it's amaz-

ing to hear so many people deny their mortality with "That won't happen to me."

2. They're "too" busy, or having too much fun to take time to prepare the most basic estate planning. "I've a good umpteen years before I need to think about that," they say, believing, "If you don't think about it, it won't happen." In the vast majority of cases, death comes as a surprise. It's sad to know that with a few minutes of planning, they could have spared their loved ones a lot of grief and money.

3. Finally, there is the Rhett Butler philosophy. It goes like this: "Frankly, my dear, I don't give a damn!" Yes, there are folks who for one reason or another just don't care about what happens to those they leave behind—wives, children, or even aged parents. If you make no plans and the inevitable happens, you will pass away *intestate*. Simply put, it means a person who dies without leaving a will. If this happens to you, the courts must decide who your heirs are and how they share your estate.

Don't complain in the hereafter that it's not what you would have chosen. You gave away control of your estate because you didn't care. Control is now vested in the probate court. The court's distribution plans are set by state law with little or no concern for the interests of your family. It benefits no one should you die intestate—not your family, your heirs, and not even the probate court, which is usually overloaded and bogged down. The only ones who really benefit are the lawyers in the form of legal fees in payment for carrying out the court's choices.

A Hollywood Tragedy

Marilyn Monroe's estate can provide an excellent example of excessive probate fees. She died in 1962 with very little estate planning other than a short, simple will. Monroe's estate was valued at approximately $100,000 at the time of her passing. She was also in debt. Over the years, however, her estate received over $1,600,000 in income from residual film payments and royalties.

In 1980, *eighteen years* after her death, the executor of Marilyn Monroe's estate settled her probate. Her heirs divided a little over $100,000 as their total inheritance. However, her real "beneficiaries" were the lawyers who represented her estate. They split over $1,000,000 in probate fees. That's ten times the amount that her loved ones received. Granted, her estate was more complex to settle than yours might be.

There is something terribly wrong with a system that provides for the interests of the lawyer over those of the rightful heirs.

If your estate falls under the jurisdiction of the probate court, consider Marilyn Monroe's estate as a very good example of the abuses, waste, and anguish that a lack of estate planning can create for the heirs. It's rare when probate doesn't cost more than anticipated and take longer.

Joint Tenancy Laws and Probate

What about joint tenancy laws? If you hold property as a joint tenant (a form of partnership) with another person, and that person passes away, will that property, and you, be protected from probate? The answer is yes . . . and no. Under joint tenancy laws, when one person passes away, those assets, held in a joint tenancy, will pass to the surviving joint tenant without the probate process. This is because the surviving joint tenant has a *right of survivor* to that particular asset. If a husband and wife own their home as joint tenants, there will be no probate needed on that home when the first spouse passes away. It will simply transfer to the surviving spouse automatically. That spouse may then file an affidavit of death of joint tenant with the county recorder or clerk to remove the name of the deceased spouse from the deed to that home.

Sounds simple enough. However, caution is the rule of the day when you hold title as a joint tenant:

1. Joint tenancy will not protect the estate of the surviving joint tenant from probate when the second person dies. In reality, joint tenant ownership merely *defers* probate until the death of the surviving joint tenant. At that time, all those assets will go straight to the probate court.

2. Joint tenant ownership takes preference over the beneficiary in your will as to who inherits the asset. For example, if you own a property as joint tenants with

24

your friend John, but the will names your brother Edward as your heir for that asset, John receives your share of the property when you pass away. Your brother Edward will have no claim on "his" share. He will have been inadvertently disinherited.

3. Your "partner" can end or break the joint tenancy by selling his/her share. Then you end up owning that asset with a "partner" you didn't select. This could result in undue stress in the relationship that might compel you to "dump" your share of the ownership in a down market. Or your new "partner" may make the relationship difficult, thus forcing you to sell your interest to him at a low price. It's quite common for someone to be forced out of an investment because of an unscrupulous "partner" or, worse, an unthinking spouse or friend.

4. The creditors of one joint tenant may attach his/her share, thereby negatively impacting the whole asset held in joint tenancy. If this happens, a court of law may order a "forced sale" of that asset (usually at a distressed price) to satisfy the creditor's judgment. This unfortunately occurs frequently. In one case, a widow put her home in joint tenancy with her son to avoid probate, only to have the home sold from underneath her because of a judgment against the son (a business failure). It's sad when something like this happens, but that's the law.

We are a nation of laws, not of justice, and there is a big difference between the two.

5. In some instances, a joint tenancy may inadvertently create a taxable gift to the partner. For example: Mr. Watson, a widower, transfers his home into joint tenancy with his daughter in an attempt to avoid probate when he passes away. He isn't aware that he has

made a "gift" of one-half of the value of that property. If the value of this "gift" exceeds $10,000, Uncle Sam may be knocking on Mr. Watson's door demanding a 37 percent gift tax on the value exceeding $10,000 (a parent may gift a child or grandchild up to $10,000 each, once a year, tax free). Mr. Watson may have to sell assets to pay those taxes. Gift taxes do not apply to joint tenancy transfers between husband and wife.

6. If your joint tenant becomes incapacitated due to an accident or medical condition, it may create difficulties. For example, if the property must be sold to generate cash to pay expenses, who will sign on behalf of the incapacitated joint tenant? If this person has not previously designated a conservator and/or attorney-in-fact, then the probate court will designate one. In either case, it will require full consent of the designee to complete the sale. Valuable time may be lost while awaiting consent. What happens if the designee doesn't agree to a sale? You are obliged to start renegotiating, or give up valuable control of the asset.

7. Finally, there are serious *income tax* consequences with the joint tenant method of holding title. These consequences could be costly to your heirs. This will be delved into later.

Distribution Technique

II. USE OF A WILL

The second method of distributing your estate is to have a typical *will* drawn up. Two questions that should concern you are:

1. What is a will?
2. What functions does it perform?

Recently, a client recommended me to a friend who had a will drawn up by a lawyer. She was charged $450 and told she was "all set," that her modest estate was in order. This person was a little shocked when I explained what her brand-new will (see below) actually was, though there are instances when a will is in order when coupled with other estate planning.

A will is nothing more than *instructions* to the probate court. That's the only function it has. It tells the probate court judge how you want your estate distributed to your beneficiaries. However, the probate court judge can throw out your will and substitute it with a court-imposed plan of distribution. The probate court is *not* bound by the distribution instructions in your will.

A will does not protect your estate from unnecessary inheritance taxes. Also, it does not protect your estate from income taxes. *It is not designed to accomplish these goals.* In order to provide that protection, you need appropriate estate planning tools.

Everyone knows the Ten Commandments. Few, however, know the "Eleventh" Commandment, which is "If you have a will, thou shalt go through probate." A will and probate are synonymous.

WILL CONSIDERATIONS

There are several considerations to take into account when deciding whether to use a typical will to provide for the distribution of your estate.

The first consideration is that of "control." The typical will can provide you with "control" on how you want your estate distributed among your heirs—provided the probate court agrees and your will is not challenged. You can specify who is to receive a favorite piece of jewelry or family heirloom.

Unlike passing away intestate, wherein the court will determine who gets what and when, a will helps you "control" the distribution of your estate. I have put the word *control* in quotation marks because the will may be wasted if your estate is challenged by an unhappy heir. One-third of all wills are challenged by brothers and/or sisters after a parent passes away. A will is no guarantee that your wishes will be honored. The probate court will think nothing of throwing out your directions and superseding them with its own, or those of a third party.

A will does not reduce or avoid taxes or other fees that may be assessed against your estate. As stated earlier, a will is not designed to deal with those issues; it only guarantees that your estate will be probated.

Distribution Technique

III. TRUSTS

The way to legally transfer your estate to your heirs after your passing is for you (and your spouse) to establish a *trust*.

Since properly drawn trusts offer significant advantages over the other two estate planning methods of distribution—(1) a will or (2) no will—trusts, and *revocable living trusts* in particular, may provide the best solution to fulfilling your estate planning needs and goals.

There has always been a great deal of information (unpublicized) about trusts, and the living trust, among affluent members of our society. But in recent years, this subject has been "popularized" and this popularity has created a lot of misinformation and half-truths. The following should clear the air about trusts—what they are, what they can or can't do, and when not to use them.

The essence of sound estate planning is knowing your options so you can use the best tools to satisfy your individual needs and goals.

The Living Trust

A living trust is a legal entity created by law. All states have the right, under the United States Constitution, to create legal entities that include partnerships, corporations . . . and trusts. A trust's purpose is to hold assets for the benefit of a person or group. Why have your hard-earned assets owned by a legal entity? The answer is quite simple. You will create a living trust because of the following reasons:

1. Your estate will not come under the jurisdiction of the probate court, lawyers, third parties, or other outsiders. Your chosen family members or friends will be empowered to carry out your wishes as per the written instructions set forth in your living trust. You may also designate the trust department of a bank, or a trust administration company, as your "successor trustee." The annual fee for professionals to perform this service averages from .5 to 1 percent of the value of the trust estate.

2. You can minimize fees and gain important tax benefits. There can be significant income tax benefits as well as federal inheritance tax benefits by having your assets in a revocable living trust. You can achieve a full "stepped-up valuation" on your capital assets (home, stocks, etc.) so that your heir(s) may inherit these assets income tax free!

3. Even if you become incapacitated, remember that a living trust, above all, is a device by which you *maintain control of your estate while you are alive*. This control

can continue for many years after your passing (particularly if it involves children).

One woman stipulated that her daughter could not take title to the real estate, left to her in trust, for thirty years from the date of the mother's death. Extreme? Perhaps. Yet, this is a good example of the degree of control you can have with a living trust. Another client had an adult son with a drug addiction problem. Our client was able to set up conditions through her living trust whereby the son had to pass successive random drug tests before any funds would be released to him.

You can set up a living trust so that if you become incapacitated and unable to manage your own affairs, the trust can shield you from losing control of your estate to outsiders or greedy family members.

4. A trust will help to keep your family's affairs private. Unlike a will, your estate under a living trust will not become a matter of public record. Your assets and your heirs will remain private.

5. You can avoid the problems associated with joint tenant ownership. As stated earlier, in some instances, joint tenant ownership can be a trap, leaving you without full control of your assets and even ownership of those assets. There are serious pitfalls in holding title to assets as joint tenants. The property could become subject to creditor claims, left to unintended heirs, create gift taxation, or be subjected to unfavorable income taxes upon your passing.

A properly drawn and funded living trust will accomplish the above five items, plus a lot more.

How the Living Trust Works

How is the living trust able to provide so many advantages in estate planning? When you set up a living trust, you simply transfer the title or ownership of all your assets into your living trust, to be controlled by the trustee(s) of that trust.

All those assets that you owned in your name as an individual, or married couple, will now be owned by your trust. You no longer own anything.

Right about now you may be getting a little nervous. People usually do when they no longer own anything. This happens because they equate change of ownership with loss of control. Be assured that while you are trustee(s) of your own revocable living trust, you will have the same control as you do today. Your lifestyle need not change. If you want to sell your home, sell it. If you want to open up bank accounts, do so. If you want to buy stocks or bonds, go ahead. If you want to spend each and every last dime, spend it. The choice is yours.

Simply stated, you are no longer the "owner" of your estate assets, which were transferred into the trust. Legally, your living trust is the "owner" of those assets. But as trustee(s) of your revocable living trust, *you maintain full control over all your trust's assets*. You may even give away some or all the assets.

It's the living trust's ownership of your assets that provides you with the ability to avoid probate legally. As an individual, you own nothing. Consequently, upon your passing (or, in the case of a married couple, the passing of either spouse), there is no need to remove your name or your spouse's from those assets through the probate court. Probate is avoided completely.

Many Hats to Wear

A trust is a legal entity, a "paper person," so to speak. As such, that "paper person" can do nothing on its own. It needs a manager or administrator to take control. Someone to make things happen. That someone is called a trustee. Just as a captain has complete control over a ship at sea, a trustee has complete control over the management of a living trust and its assets.

The person who sets up the living trust, creates the "paper person," and determines the powers to be vested in it is referred to as the trustor.

Also involved in the trust is the settlor, who is responsible for transferring ownership of assets into the trust. This transfer is called *funding* the trust.

It is critical that your living trust "own" your assets. You must fund your trust in order to activate its powers. An unfunded trust is merely an empty shell that will give your heirs no protection. Funding your trust is a simple process.

Finally, there is the beneficiary for whom the living trust is created. He/she is the recipient of the trust assets, income, enjoyment of, and rights thereto.

Who Are All These People?

Before you get too concerned about the different people having control and rights over your assets, here are their identities:

The TRUSTOR is YOU! Yes, with a properly drawn living trust, *you* are allowed to be the trustor and set up your own living trust. By doing so, you determine the character of the living trust document as well as the final allocation and distribution of your estate.

The SETTLOR is YOU! You also are allowed to be the settlor and "fund" your own living trust with your assets. This includes all your major assets, such as real estate, bank accounts, stocks, bonds, mutual funds, insurance proceeds, cars, and all other form and nature of assets. The Internal Revenue Service refers to the settlor as the grantor. They are one and the same.

The TRUSTEE is YOU! In addition, you are allowed to name yourself trustee of your living trust and therefore have absolute control of all the assets in your trust. The day-to-day management of your affairs will not change.

The BENEFICIARY is YOU! While you are alive, you are allowed to be your own beneficiary. You are setting up a living trust, and putting assets into it for your beneficial use and enjoyment. It is only after you pass away that your primary beneficiaries, or heirs, receive their inheritance as per the instructions in your trust.

Maximizing Estate Planning: Using an A-B Married Revocable Living Trust

The above information can be applied to an A-type single (individual) revocable living trust or an A-type married (couple) revocable living trust.

Here is an estate planning strategy, which can be used by any married couple, to pass up to $1,200,000 tax free to their heirs. This strategy centers on you and your spouse creating an A-B married revocable living trust.

It begins like an A married revocable living trust. You and your spouse set up a living trust and "fund" it with your assets. As the managers and administrators of the trust estate, you can buy, sell, and in all other ways control your assets just as you do right now. The difference between an A married revocable living trust and an A-B married revocable living trust does not come into the picture until one spouse passes away. Then the extra estate planning protection of the A-B married revocable living trust becomes apparent.

With the first spouse gone, this type of living trust divides into two separate parts: the survivor's "Trust A" and the deceased's "B Trust." It does not matter whether husband or wife passes away first, the A and B designations remain the same. The assets of the surviving spouse, made up of his or her separate property and one-half of the commonly owned property, are assigned to Trust A. The other one-half of the commonly owned property and all of the decedent's separate property are then assigned to the B Trust *without* the need for probate. The surviving spouse has complete management control over Trust A. If so stipulated, the surviving spouse also may have complete control over the assets in the B Trust.

The IRS rules and regulations allow the surviving spouse three very important benefits concerning his or her ability to use those assets in the B Trust.

First, the surviving spouse can spend all of the income (if any) generated by the assets in the B Trust to maintain his/her standard of living. This could be rent from real estate, stock dividends, interest, disbursements, and even business income. If that income is not enough to maintain the surviving spouse's standard of living, the surviving spouse has the additional following benefit.

The surviving spouse also can have full access to all of the B Trust's principal if needed for health care, general support, and maintenance of his/her standard of living. All it means exactly is that he/she can spend every last penny if needed.

The third right given to the surviving spouse is that he/she can draw $5,000, or 5 percent of the principal, once a year from the B Trust: the surviving spouse can take a vacation, give it away, or even go to Las Vegas. Uncle Sam doesn't care. This access is referred to as the "frivolous right."

Upon the death of the surviving spouse, the assets of both A and B parts of the trust come back together and pass to your beneficiaries. These assets completely avoid the probate process as it passes to the surviving spouse and *again* when it passes to your heirs. Thus, two probates are completely avoided.

Why divide the estate? This division of the estate into

two trusts, A and B, takes advantage of some important IRS inheritance tax laws. If each Trust A and B Trust contains less then $600,000, these assets will pass to your heirs federal inheritance tax free. Thus, an A-B married revocable living trust enables you to benefit from *both* husband's and wife's personal estate exemptions and transfer to your heirs up to $1,200,000 without federal inheritance tax.

Is a Living Trust the Right Solution for Me?

Estate planning is never a "one size fits all" strategy. It is as varied in its solutions as are the needs of the families setting them up. The secret to proper planning is having the knowledge and ability to employ the right tool for the right job. You don't use a handsaw to split firewood, nor drive a spike with a tack hammer. The use of an A single, A married, A-B married, or A-B-C married living trust depends on: (a) the anticipated value of the estate at the passing of the individual or first spouse; (b) distribution questions; (c) family control; and (d) allocation issues.

These documents are designed to fulfill three definite tasks. To:

1. Avoid probate.
2. Maintain privacy and family control.
3. Obtain certain tax benefits.

The value of a living trust depends on your given situation, plus your needs and goals. And as useful as it is, the living trust is not always the best instrument to use in every situation.

There are circumstances in which a living trust is inappropriate for the job you want done. The following examples will not detail joint tenant ownership with right of survivor to "avoid" probate. Joint tenancy only defers probate to the surviving joint tenant. It is discussed at length in other sections of this book.

When No Probate Is Required

Consider the following situation in which probate would not be required on a decedent's assets and a living trust would be unnecessary.

Mr. and Mrs. Hoover

Mr. and Mrs. Hoover are a childless couple, residents of California. They do not own real estate, stocks, or other investments. They have a jointly owned checking account of a little less than $25,000. Mr. Hoover has a small insurance policy naming his wife as the beneficiary.

Do the Hoovers have an estate tax problem? No,

since their estate is less than $600,000, they do not have to worry about paying Uncle Sam a portion of their estate. With or without a living trust, this estate will pass to the surviving spouse free of any federal inheritance tax.

Do the Hoovers have a potential probate problem? No, their estate will avoid probate court and be shielded completely.

Upon the passing of Mr. Hoover, his wife continues control of their one asset, the checking account. She can make deposits, write checks, and even spend the account to a zero balance. Being the named beneficiary of her husband's life insurance policy, she files a claim on Mr. Hoover's $50,000 life insurance policy and deposits the proceeds into the checking account. She spends all the funds over the ensuing years and passes away as a ward of the state of California.

The Hoovers avoided probate on both the passing of husband and wife because:

1. They jointly owned and controlled their one asset, the checking account. This account was set up as an "or" account, in which either spouse could access the account, sign checks, and spend the funds as he/she saw fit. If this account had been set up as an "and" account, both signatures would have been needed to sign checks. This would have put the estate at jeopardy of probate. The "or" technique provides the surviving spouse, Mrs. Hoover, access to the bank account and thus avoids probate.

2. Assets, like life insurance, have a designated beneficiary and do not come under the jurisdiction of the probate court. Mrs. Hoover, as beneficiary of

the policy, avoided probate. She filed a claim for the death benefit when she provided a certified copy of Mr. Hoover's death certificate to the insurance carrier, and her claim was paid.

3. When Mrs. Hoover passed away destitute, there was no estate from which her name had to be removed, so probate was not required. The state of California made no claim, as there was nothing left in the Hoover estate.

Items That Will Avoid Probate

A probate estate is made up of items and assets that are transferred to the heirs under the terms, instructions, and conditions set forth in the will. If the decedent passes away intestate, the laws of the particular state where probate is "proved" will apply to this transfer.

The following items "avoid" probate because of their nature:

1. Assets gifted away outright to another individual or a trust during your lifetime.
2. Interests in trusts that terminate upon the passing of the beneficiary.
3. Assets, like a bank account, held "in trust for." These accounts are referred to as Totten trusts. A word of caution regarding this type of account. Though this type of trust account *should* avoid probate, nevertheless, some banks request a "court order" to release funds held in this manner.

The term *court order* is a code phrase that means "probate."

4. Life insurance proceeds payable to specified beneficiaries, other than to the estate.

5. Assets held in joint tenant ownership, with right of survivor. Caution! There are negative aspects to this form of ownership (outlined elsewhere).

6. Annuity contracts and retirement plans that are payable to a surviving or named beneficiary.

Summary Probate

Every state sets a level of valuation below which there is no need for a probate in order to pass the decedent's estate to his/her heirs. If, at the time of your passing, your personal estate is inventoried and appraised at a value below the probate threshold, your heirs will inherit the estate free from probate. Property you own in a state other than your residence requires appraisal of assets in the second state. If the established value falls below that state's valuation threshold, your estate will also avoid probate in that state.

Under these conditions, you may be able to file a petition for summary probate. This is a simple process—a mini-probate, as it were—by which an accounting and affidavit of worth are filed with the probate court. If there is no challenge or creditor claims made within the statutory time frame, the judge will "rubber stamp" the petition as accepted and this mini-probate will have been quickly, and simply, completed.

At that point, the assets can be distributed to the heirs and the estate settled.

A petition for summary probate requires one to two months to complete and costs several hundred dollars to file. The following is an example of a summary or mini-probate.

Mr. Freeman

Mr. Freeman, a single man (divorced), is a resident of the state of Iowa. He owns an undeveloped building lot in a rural area in the southern part of the state of South Carolina. It is valued at $8,000 and he plans to construct, someday, a small retirement cabin. His other assets include some stock shares, a checking and a savings account, and personal property. The value of his assets, excluding real estate, is $45,000. His estate will never exceed $53,000. His one grown son is his heir.

Does Mr. Freeman's son have an estate tax problem?

No. As the assets have a value of less than $600,000, he doesn't have to worry about paying a portion of the estate to Uncle Sam. With or without a living trust, the estate will pass to the son free of any federal inheritance tax.

Does Mr. Freeman have a potential probate problem?

No. The estate will avoid a full probate court proceeding and pass to the son in a short period of time.

The procedure. After the passing of Mr. Freeman, his son files a petition for summary probate with the clerks of the probate courts in both states of residence, Iowa and South Carolina. He obtains a quote on the value of his father's stock from a local broker, provides an ending balance on the bank accounts, and itemizes the personal property.

In South Carolina, he hires an appraiser to place a value on the building site. He delivers to the court in each state a certified copy of his father's death certificate, pays a small filing fee, provides proof that his father was sole owner of those assets, proves he is his father's child and heir, and signs an affidavit under oath, subject to penalty for perjury, that the accounting and assets value of his father's estate are true and correct.

Approximately two months later, both petitions are accepted by the courts in both states, and the primary and the ancillary summary proceedings are closed. Mr. Freeman's son obtains the balance of his father's estate.

Mr. Freeman's estate avoided full probate because the value of his assets at the time of death were below the probate thresholds set by the two states. As such, his estate qualified for the relatively simple process of summary probate.

Total time? Two months.

Total expenses? Under $1,000.

Probate Can Be Advantageous

Yes, in some situations, probate may be the best solution. Probate is a process controlled by the court. As such, some beneficiaries feel "protected" under court control, believing their best interests are being served. It can go a long way in providing a sense that "justice" is being rendered.

Prior to a release of assets to the heirs, the court, in most jurisdictions, is required to enter a decree of distribution. The heirs will execute receipts for the assets willed to them, and these receipts are filed with the court. Unfortunately, this sense of security is sometimes shattered. It is shattered because of the abuses common in many probate proceedings; the cost "overruns," time extensions, endless paperwork, greedy or unintended heirs, and a system that cares little for the pain you are experiencing at the loss of a loved one.

Another advantage to subjecting the estate to probate comes in its ability to dismiss creditor claims. During a probate, notices to creditors are posted. Any claim against the estate must be filed with the court in order for that debt to be included in the proceeding. These claims must be filed within a statutory time frame. Failure to do so prevents a creditor from *ever* collecting his or her debt. The assets will pass to the heirs debt free.

These "advantages" may not be worthwhile when compared with the disadvantages of a full probate process, involving the cost, loss of privacy, and frustration of dealing with bureaucracy.

Estate Planning Case Studies

Let's examine the case studies of four estates: Ms. Sara Douglas, the Baker family, the Sheltons, and the Dumont family. Each case has specific problems and uses a revocable living trust structured to the individual and family needs to solve those problems.

Ms. Douglas

Meet Ms. Sara Douglas, a single woman. She has two minor children. Her estate is valued at $400,000, and consists of her home, a bond fund to provide for her children's college educations, simple checking and savings accounts, and a rare coin collection given to her by her father. For our purposes, her estate will be free of federal inheritance tax.

Does Ms. Douglas have a potential probate problem?

Yes. Because of the large sum, her estate is headed for probate—unless she does some simple estate planning.

Her goal is to conserve as much of the estate as possible for her children, to provide for their care, and, ultimately, to pass on the remainder of the estate to them.

DOUGLAS ESTATE
$400,000

WILL or INTESTATE

LIVING TRUST

$400,000

$400,000

PROBATE FEES

$32,000

TRUST A

$400,000 FOR HER CHILDREN

$368,000

NET FOR HER HEIRS

$400,000

$32,000 MORE FOR HEIRS

MS. DOUGLAS'S SOLUTION

The solution Ms. Douglas found to be in everyone's best interest was to create a simple A-type single revocable living trust. She transferred all her assets, including her home, into this trust and named herself trustee of the Sara Douglas Trust. As such, she retains complete control of the assets. She names her brother, George, successor trustee, to take control of the trust at her passing. The trust specifies the allocation (what assets her children are to inherit) and the distribution (when her children are to receive their share of the assets).

How it works: Upon her death, the successor trustee takes control of the trust estate without going through probate. During the ensuing years, the brother manages the assets for the benefit of Sara's two children, and provides living and medical expenses. The college fund provides for their college educations. When each child turns twenty-five, the brother will distribute the remaining assets to each one. Without interruption, the Douglas children have received proper care, education, and, finally, all the assets of the Sara Douglas Trust as she had intended.

MS. DOUGLAS'S BENEFITS

What Ms. Douglas gained by creating an A-type single revocable living trust:

1. She retained control of her assets during her lifetime.
2. If she became incapacitated, her successor trustee could have stepped in to manage her affairs without going through a court-appointed conservator.

3. When Ms. Douglas passed away, her estate avoided probate. Estimated savings to the Douglas children, $32,000.*

4. In addition, she was able to obtain a 100 percent "stepped up" basis on her capital assets, such as her real estate and rare coin collection. These assets will then pass to her children income tax free.

Mr. and Mrs. Baker

Mr. and Mrs. Baker are a married couple in their mid-fifties with four grown children. Their estate is valued at about $300,000, and is made up of their home, a stock fund account, and checking and savings accounts. For our purposes, their estate carries this value upon the death of the first spouse.

Do the Bakers have an estate tax problem? No. Since their estate is less than $600,000, they do not have to worry about losing a portion of their estate to Uncle Sam. With or without a living trust, the estate will pass to the surviving spouse and subsequently to their children free of any federal inheritance tax.

* Probate savings are arrived at by adding the average California lawyer's fees and estate executor's fees. The fees were provided by independent sources and are in line with the average amount charged in most states. The fees and costs do not include any special fees or commissions paid on the sale of assets or possible litigation. Probate fees in states vary. Readers are encouraged to seek information as to the specific fees and costs in the state of residence, and other states where property is located. All values used in this example are rounded to the nearest $100.

Do the Bakers have a potential probate problem? Yes. The estate is headed for the probate court unless they do some rather simple estate planning.

At the passing of the first spouse, the goal was to pass the assets to the surviving spouse without probate, and subsequently to their children, at the passing of the surviving spouse. Probate was avoided not just once (as with joint tenant ownership), but twice.

MR. AND MRS. BAKER'S SOLUTION

The Bakers created a simple, type A married revocable living trust and transferred all their assets (including their home) into it. They named themselves trustees of the Baker Family Trust. As such, they retained complete control of the assets. When they set up their revocable living trust, they named their oldest child, Virginia, successor trustee. In addition, they provided for the allocation (what portion of the assets each child was to inherit) and the distribution (when each child was to receive his/her share of the estate) in the living trust document.

The mechanics of the trust: When the first spouse passes away, the surviving spouse controls the Baker Family Trust. He/she will continue to receive the income generated by the trust and be able to sell assets, change the nature of assets, or acquire new assets in the Baker Family Trust.

The surviving spouse avoids the emotional agony and wasted cost of going through probate.

When the surviving spouse dies, Virginia, the successor trustee, takes over management of the trust assets without going through probate. Without inter-

BAKER ESTATE
$300,000

WILL or INTESTATE

LIVING TRUST

$150,000 $150,000

$150,000 $150,000

PROBATE FEES

$12,000

TRUST A

$288,000 FOR
SURVIVING SPOUSE

$300,000 FOR
SURVIVING SPOUSE

PROBATE FEES

$23,000

$265,000

**NET FOR
THEIR HEIRS**

$300,000

**$35,000 MORE
FOR HEIRS**

ruption, the Baker children will receive all the property and assets of the Baker Family Trust.

MR. AND MRS. BAKER'S BENEFITS

This is what Mr. and Mrs. Baker gained by creating an A married revocable living trust:

1. After the passing of the first spouse, the surviving spouse remained in control of the estate. After the surviving spouse passed away, the family maintained control. All this without probate.
2. There was additional protection in case they both became incapacitated. In this event, the successor trustee could step in and manage their affairs until one or both recovered, without requiring a court-appointed conservator.
3. The Baker children avoided probate twice after the passing of each parent. Estimated savings to the Baker family, $35,000.*
4. In addition, Mr. and Mrs. Baker obtained a 100 percent "stepped-up basis" on all their capital assets, such as real estate and stocks. These assets then passed to their children income tax free.

---

* Probate savings are arrived at by adding the average lawyer's fees and estate executor's fees. The California average fees, which, as provided by independent sources, are the average amount charged in most states, were used to calculate above fees. These do not include any special fees, such as commissions paid on the sale of assets, tax preparation costs, and possible litigation. Probate fees in all states vary, and the reader is encouraged to seek local sources for information as to the specific fees and costs that may apply in their state of residence, and other states where property may be situated. For the purpose of convenience, all values used in this example have been rounded to the nearest $100.

Mr. and Mrs. Shelton

Let's look at another case, Mr. and Mrs. Shelton. They also have grown children. The Sheltons have an estate worth $1,000,000. It comprises their home, investment real estate, a diversified stock portfolio, and several cash accounts. Their estate is debt free. Again, for our purposes, their estate will not be increasing.

Do the Sheltons have an estate tax problem? Yes, since their estate is over $600,000, they will have a significant inheritance tax liability unless they plan their estate properly.

Do the Sheltons have a potential probate problem?

Yes, unless they plan and provide the means whereby the estate will pass to their children, shielded from probate.

Their goal is to pass the estate to their heirs, free of estate taxes, free of income taxes, and without the time and expense of probate.

MR. AND MRS. SHELTON'S SOLUTION

Because their estate has a value of $1,000,000, Mr. and Mrs. Shelton decide to establish an A-B married revocable living trust and transfer their assets into the trust. They name themselves as the trustees of the Shelton Family Trust, with complete control over the trust assets. They name their two oldest children, Ruth and Harold, as successor co-trustees to take over control of the trust after they both pass away. They also provide for the allocation of shares or assets each child is to inherit and the distribution of the estate.

How it works: Upon the passing of the first spouse, the surviving spouse retains control of the Shelton Family Trust as the surviving trustee; this includes the right to sell assets, change the nature of assets, or acquire new assets in the name of the trust, and he/she continues to receive the income generated by the trust assets. At this time, two "separate" trusts are created with the surviving spouse still in control of all assets.

One-half of all the jointly owned property and any assets owned as separate property of the surviving spouse will be transferred to Trust A. Its value is $500,000. The other half of the jointly owned property and any assets owned as separate property of the deceased spouse will be transferred into the B Trust. Its value is $500,000. This creates two separate entities, each of which is entitled to use a $600,000 personal estate exemption.

Since the B Trust estate of the deceased spouse has a $600,000 exemption, the estate won't owe any federal inheritance tax. *All* of those funds are now safe from probate and any inheritance tax, and in the future as well. This is because Uncle Sam values an estate using only the date of death to establish its taxable value. In fact, after this valuation has been made, the B Trust can grow in value above $600,000 and it will *never* carry an inheritance tax liability no matter what the future value may become.

The surviving spouse will continue to receive the income generated by the trust assets. He or she can sell assets, change the nature of assets, or acquire new assets in the name of the Shelton Family Trust. Any of the trust assets can be used to maintain his or her standard of living.

Uncle Sam also gives the surviving spouse a "frivo-

SHELTON ESTATE
$1,000,000

WILL or INTESTATE

LIVING TRUST

$500,000 $500,000

$500,000 $500,000

PROBATE FEES
$40,000

TRUST B — TRUST A

$500,000 $500,000

$960,000 FOR
SURVIVING SPOUSE

$1,000,000 FOR
SURVIVING SPOUSE

PROBATE
FEES &
TAXES *
$184,000

$776,000
NET FOR
THEIR HEIRS

$1,000,000

$224,000 MORE FOR HEIRS

* FEDERAL INHERITANCE TAX ONLY

lous" right to spend a portion of the trust estate on anything he or she might decide to do—take a vacation to Europe, for example.

Upon the passing of the surviving spouse, the assets of both A and B trusts come back together and pass to the Shelton children. The successor co-trustees will take over control of the trust estate, without probate, and distribute those assets to the beneficiaries of Mr. and Mrs. Shelton. Simply and quietly, without intrusion, the Shelton children remain in control of the family fortune.

Since the Trust A and B Trust are each under the $600,000 personal estate exemption level, the entire trust estate and its assets valued at $1,000,000 will pass to the Shelton children inheritance tax free.

MR. AND MRS. SHELTON'S BENEFITS

This is what Mr. and Mrs. Shelton have gained by creating an A-B married revocable living trust:

1. They maintain complete control over their assets during both their lifetimes. They are free to do whatever they want with their assets; after both pass away, their family retains control of the estate.
2. In the event that they should become incapacitated, their successor co-trustees can step in and manage their affairs until they recover, without having to go through a court-appointed conservator.
3. After the deaths of both Mr. and Mrs. Shelton, the estate will have avoided probate twice. Estimated savings to the Shelton family: $116,800.

4. By creating an A-B married living trust, Mr. and Mrs. Shelton were able to take advantage of both of their $600,000 personal estate exemptions, thus allowing them to allocate their entire estate to their children, inheritance tax free. Estimated estate tax savings to the Shelton family: $107,200.

   Estimated combined probate and estate tax savings to the Shelton family: $224,000.*

5. In addition, Mr. and Mrs. Shelton were able to obtain a 100 percent "stepped-up basis" on all of their capital assets, including real estate and stocks. These assets then pass to their children income tax free.

Mr. and Mrs. Dumont

We now have the case of Mr. and Mrs. Dumont. Their estate has a value of $3,000,000. It comprises their

---

* The above estate tax amount assumes that the Sheltons will use the unified tax credit equivalent. Probate savings are arrived at by adding the lawyer's fees and estate executor's fees. The California average fees, which, as provided by independent sources, are the average amount charged in most states, were used to calculate the above fees. These do not include any special fees, such as commissions paid on the sale of assets, tax preparation costs, and possible litigation. Probate fees in all states vary, and the reader is encouraged to seek local sources for information as to the specific fees and costs as they may apply in their specific state of residence, and other states where property may be situated. For the purpose of convenience, all values used in this example have been rounded to the nearest $100.

primary home, a vacation home, investment real estate, a diversified stock portfolio, high-yield bond funds, income-generating secured debt, life insurance, and several cash accounts. They also own and operate their own business. Their children are grown. For our purposes, their estate will not be increasing in value.

Have the Dumonts an estate tax problem? Yes, since their estate is over $600,000, they will have a significant federal inheritance tax liability unless they plan their estate properly.

In addition, the Dumonts have a probate problem unless they do some estate planning to provide for the means whereby the estate will pass to the surviving spouse and then to their children shielded from probate.

Their goal is to pass the estate to their heirs, with a minimum federal inheritance tax liability, yet still pass on their assets free of income taxes on capital gains, and without the time and expense of probate.

MR. AND MRS. DUMONT'S SOLUTION

Because their estate has a value of $3,000,000, Mr. and Mrs. Dumont establish an A-B-C (QTIP or Qualified Terminable Interest Property Trust) married revocable living trust, commonly known as an A-B-C trust. They transfer all their assets into a trust and name themselves trustees, thus maintaining control over the assets. As they have the right to choose the name, they call it the Dumont Twenty-first Century Trust. Their three children are named successor co-trustees to control the trust after their parents pass away. In addition, they provide for the allocation (what shares or specific assets each child is to inherit) and its distribution (when their children are to receive their allocated assets) of the estate in the living trust document.

Upon the passing of the first spouse, the surviving spouse will retain full control of the management of the Dumonts' trust estate. He or she will continue to receive all income generated by the trust assets and have the right to sell assets, change the nature of assets, and even acquire new assets in the name of the Dumont Twenty-first Century Trust. The surviving spouse continues as the sole surviving trustee.

However, at this point, the A-B-C trust divides into three "separate" trusts. Trust A belongs to the surviving spouse, and includes half of the value of all jointly owned property, plus any "separate" property owned by the surviving spouse. All this ($1,500,000) is now in Trust A.

The second half of the jointly owned assets (the other $1,500,000) is divided, with $600,000 being placed into the deceased spouse's Trust B and the remaining $900,000 flowing into C Trust. There are now three "separate" trust estates, or divisions of the Dumonts' trust.

Since the Trust B estate of the deceased spouse is not more than the $600,000 exemption, the estate doesn't owe any federal inheritance tax now or in the future because Uncle Sam values an estate at the date of passing. After valuation, Trust B can grow in value above $600,000, and no matter how large this trust division grows, it will never have an inheritance tax liability.

The surviving spouse will continue to receive the income generated by the trust assets. He or she can sell assets, change the nature of assets, or even acquire new assets in the name of the Dumont Twenty-first Century Trust. Any and all of the trust assets may be used to maintain his or her standard of living and well-being, even if the entire estate in the three trusts is spent.

Uncle Sam also gives the surviving spouse the "frivolous" right to spend $5,000, or 5 percent of the principal balance of the estate, on anything at all.

Upon the passing of the surviving spouse, assets in the A, B, and C trusts are restored into a single trust. The successor co-trustees take control of the trust estate, without probate, and distribute the remainder of the estate to the heirs (the Dumont children). Simply and without intrusion, the Dumont children remain in control of the family fortune.

The differences between an A-B living trust and an A-B-C living trust are twofold:

1. If you are using an A-B married living trust when the first spouse dies, and your estate is valued at over $1,200,000, the family will owe federal inheritance taxes on every dollar over this amount. These taxes *must* be paid to the IRS within nine months after the passing of the *first* spouse and the government doesn't care where the money comes from. This may put a heavy financial burden (such as selling the house) on the surviving spouse if assets have to be sold to pay Uncle Sam his "fair share."

2. With an A-B-C living trust, the tax hassle, and other negative ramifications for the surviving spouse, can be avoided. The protection against being taxed is the foundation of the C, or QTIP, portion provided by this type of trust instrument.

Under Internal Revenue Service codes, the C division of the A-B-C living trust is not taxed until the passing of the *surviving* spouse. All the funds placed into the C Trust at the passing of the first spouse can be retained

DUMONT ESTATE
$3,000,000

WILL or INTESTATE

LIVING TRUST

$1,500,000 $1,500,000

$1,500,000 $1,500,000

PROBATE FEES & TAXES *

$120,000

$2,880,000 FOR SURVIVING SPOUSE

TRUST B   TRUST C   TRUST A

$600,000 $900,000 $1,500,000

$3,000,000 FOR SURVIVING SPOUSE

PROBATE FEES & TAXES *

$1,140,000

MAXIMUM ESTATE TAXES *

$785,000

$1,740,000
NET FOR THEIR HEIRS

$2,215,000

$475,000 MORE FOR HEIRS

* FEDERAL INHERITANCE TAX ONLY

for the benefit of the surviving spouse. This can provide a significant financial advantage at a time when he or she may need it most for general support and maintenance of lifestyle.

It is only after the surviving spouse has passed away that the federal government will demand that taxes be paid. This is where the second major benefit of the QTIP trust is realized.

As you will remember, under the Dumont Twenty-first Century Trust, $900,000 in assets were placed into the C Trust. The surviving spouse had access to the funds for his or her well-being, and, as such, part of the estate was depleted. The C Trust now contains less than the amount that went into it initially. Upon the passing of the second spouse, an accounting of that C Trust will be made for federal inheritance tax purposes.

Although Uncle Sam's share is now due, *the IRS can tax only what remains in the C Trust, NOT the original $900,000 that went into it.* If the assets in the C Trust (QTIP) were spent totally to support the surviving spouse, and Trust A was spent down to under $600,000, there are no federal inheritance taxes due. The IRS treats the C Trust as a gift under the unlimited marital deduction, and the surviving spouse retains the personal estate exemption. The Dumont family paid no federal inheritance taxes whatsoever on an estate of $3,000,000.

This was accomplished because they took direct action by using the power of the A-B-C (QTIP) married revocable living trust to achieve significant tax savings.

MR. AND MRS. DUMONT'S BENEFITS

This is what Mr. and Mrs. Dumont gained by creating an A-B-C (QTIP) revocable living trust:

1. They maintained control over their assets during their lifetimes. After both passed away, their family maintained control of the estate.
2. In the event they became incapacitated, their successor co-trustees could step in to manage their affairs until they recovered, without having a court-appointed conservator.
3. The Dumont family avoided probate twice on the deaths of both Mr. and Mrs. Dumont, saving the family an estimated $292,000.
4. By creating an A-B-C (QTIP) revocable living trust, Mr. and Mrs. Dumont were able to take advantage of both $600,000 personal estate exemptions, with the balance treated as a gift under the unlimited marital deduction. This allowed them to allocate their entire estate to their children, inheritance tax free. Estimated estate tax savings to the Dumonts, $889,000.

   Estimated combined probate and estate tax savings to the Dumont family, $1,181,000.*
5. Mr. and Mrs. Dumont were able to obtain a 100 percent "stepped-up basis" on all their capital assets, such as real estate and stocks. These assets then pass to their children income tax free.

---

* The above estate tax amount assumes that the Dumonts will use the unified tax credit equivalent. Probate savings are arrived at by adding the usual lawyer's fees and estate executor's fees. The California average fees, which, as provided by independent sources, are the average amount charged in most states, were used to calculate the fees. These referenced fees and costs do not include any special fees, such as commissions paid on the sale of assets, tax preparation costs, and possible litigation. Probate fees in all states vary, and the reader is encouraged to seek local sources for information as to specific fees, as they may apply in their state of residence, and other states, where their property is situated. For the purpose of convenience, all values used in this example have been rounded to the nearest $100.

Taking Control

The ability of Ms. Douglas, the Bakers, Mr. and Mrs. Shelton, and the Dumont family to avoid probate, obtain important inheritance and income tax benefits, and pass significant savings to their heirs was accomplished through the use of simple estate planning tools. No gimmicks or "tax shelters" were used to accomplish their goals.

The secret of their success is that they sat down and made their estate plans. With knowledge and the right document package, it was easy.

They not only gained thousands of dollars for their families, but they also gained peace of mind for themselves, knowing their beneficiaries would not suffer the delay and legal expense of probate.

Other Trust Options

Trusts should be an integral part of estate planning. There are numerous options available to you other than the revocable living trust. These are trusts designed to do a particular job under specific circumstances, yet they may not be applicable when the use of a simple trust would be more appropriate. If one of these forms seems right for your needs, you are urged to contact your own adviser and discuss the matter.

The Generation-Skipping Trust

This is a strategy grandparents may use to pass up to $2,000,000 to their grandchildren to be divided among them. There are three reasons why a couple might want to consider using this form of trust.

1. By removing these funds from their estate, they effectively reduce the size of that estate for tax purposes.
2. They can make certain the money will get to the rightful heirs, the grandchildren, should their own children squander their own inheritance.
3. If their children, the first generation, are likely to incur tax liabilities by obtaining these funds, that generation may be skipped and specific funds given to the grandchildren, the second generation. These assets will not be considered part of the first generation's inheritance and therefore will not create an additional tax burden.

Generation-skipping trusts are not what they used to be. Their power, and therefore their usefulness, in the transfer of large sums with few tax ramifications have been greatly reduced. Depending on how this trust is structured, there might be a larger tax bite than the amount in the trust fund itself.

The 1993 Budget Reconciliation Act began an all-out assault on this form of trust, which has been viewed as the quintessential device used by the "rich" to avoid paying their fair share. More erosion in the benefits of the generation-skipping trust is expected during the next three years.

The Testamentary Trust

This trust is referred to fondly in legal circles as the "attorney retirement plan," and lawyers often recommend this type of trust. The lawyer first charges a tidy sum to set up the testamentary trust. Then, the attorney charges you again when the estate is probated. A testamentary trust is merely a part of your will and becomes active upon your passing. The assets you thought were safe are actually forced through probate *before* they fund your testamentary trust. Since this trust is subject to probate, it is also vulnerable to being challenged in court.

A testamentary trust provides a couple with the ability to take advantage of both the husband's and wife's personal estate exemption, but at a high price.

The Charitable Remainder Trust

While the lawyer sings the praises of the testamentary trust, the insurance agent does the same for the charitable remainder trust. Here's how it works. You bestow an asset—worth $1,000,000, for example—as a gift to a charity, your old school, or a medical foundation. Because these institutions are quite sophisticated, they all prefer real estate, quality stocks, or anything likely to appreciate. In return, they will purchase a life insurance policy on your life with your heirs as beneficiaries. The face value of the policy will be equal in value to the asset at the time you gave it to them. You retain income from the asset or, in the case of real estate, a life estate in the property.

Over the years, due to normal inflation, the property will likely increase in value, while the insurance policy "decreases" in value (because the purchase power of the dollar will be decreasing). When you pass away, the charity gets an asset that may have appreciated to $1,500,000 tax free, while your heirs inherit the $1,000,000 insurance policy tax free.

Your estate benefits from the income tax breaks you receive.

The Irrevocable Trust

Caution is the watchword when you consider using this form of trust. As its name indicates, this trust cannot be changed once it is activated. Therefore, you lose control of that portion of your estate (or even all of it) that is placed in the trust. You relinquish control of the trust to a trustee other than yourself, as you can't be the trustee of your own irrevocable trust. This requirement does not apply to the "irrevocable" divisions of an A-B and A-B-C living trust.

Why set up a trust in which you lose control of all or part of your assets? Because there are several substantial benefits to a family using the irrevocable trust. Briefly:

1. If allowed under your state of residence laws, this trust can shield your estate from attachment by your creditors.
2. As you do not have the assets (primarily property) in your estate under your control, your tax liability is greatly reduced.
3. It can be used as a vehicle for holding trust funds (or even an insurance policy) allocated to minor beneficiaries.
4. Its greatest benefit (and the reason why families choose this type of trust) is its power to protect assets in the event of catastrophic illness, loss of competency, or extended nursing home care. However, the 1993 Budget Reconciliation Act has greatly diminished this benefit.

The disadvantages of this type of trust are:

1. There is no turning back once this trust is set up. If you change your mind or your situation changes, you are stuck with it.
2. Assets transferred into the trust are subject to the federal gift tax, which starts at 37 percent. The federal gift tax rate and the federal inheritance tax rate happen to be the same.

Think twice about setting up this form of trust. Obtain professional advice on your particular circumstances prior to creating a trust that cannot be altered or revoked.

The Grantor Retained Income Trust (GRIT)

This type of trust is a gamble, because if you set up a GRIT, you're betting you'll outlive the terms of the trust agreement.

Here is how it works. Gift your home—an asset that is probably your largest investment—into this trust *for a certain number of years* but retain the right to occupy the property. At the end of the specified number of years, your heirs receive the house. Sounds simple enough, but there's a catch to holding title in a GRIT.

If you expire *before* the trust expires, Uncle Sam will

tax the estate as if there were no trust at all. Taxes will be based on that property's full value as of the date you passed away.

The Qualified Domestic Trust (QDOT)

If your spouse is not a U.S. citizen, he/she will not be given the same rights in terms of certain tax benefits that a citizen receives. This trust works along the same principles as the QTIP portion of an A-B-C living trust. Your resident alien spouse is entitled to all the income generated by the assets in the QDOT trust. The major difference is that your spouse cannot be trustee of the QDOT portion; this person must be a United States citizen. You will be obliged to choose someone other than your spouse.

The Insurance Trust

This trust is a powerful tool to use as an extension to, and enhancement of, a living trust. For example:

The proceeds from your life insurance go to the beneficiary *income tax free*. Even though you never benefit directly, Uncle Sam considers this life insurance part of your estate and taxes it as such. This increased estate value could kick your estate up into a higher bracket.

For individuals who have an estate exceeding $600,000 (including a life insurance policy), and for married couples with an estate over $1,200,000 (including life insurance), there is a solution.

You might consider creating an irrevocable insurance trust. Form a trust that "owns" your life insurance policies. By using this type of trust, your life insurance is not part of your estate and therefore is not taxed as such.

Upon your death, proceeds from this insurance flow through this trust to be distributed to your beneficiaries, bypassing your estate. Your estate will not be kicked up into a higher bracket nor pay higher federal inheritance taxes.

There are three ways an estate pays estate or inheritance taxes because of the increased value of the estate:

1. When the estate is taxable, your family may have to sell an asset (for instance, your house), to pay taxes to Uncle Sam from the proceeds of that sale. The major problem with this method is that the assets you are trying to keep for your heirs will not be available. Also, market conditions may not be right for the sale of that asset, thereby producing a minimum return for your family.

2. If your family borrows money to pay the tax, your family has to repay the original (principal) amount, plus interest charges.

3. You could purchase an insurance policy for the estimated amount of the estate taxes. The proceeds from the policy cover your estate for a few

cents on each dollar, a real bargain. (NOTE: The author does not sell life insurance.) When used wisely, life insurance can be a powerful estate planning tool.

Remember, the IRS doesn't care where the "fair share" comes from, or what the family has to do to get it: the taxes are due nine months from the date of passing. If you have an A-B-C (QTIP) trust, those taxes will be deferred until the passing of the second spouse. There is an insurance policy designed to meet the needs of that particular situation called a "second to die" policy.

Even if your estate is not large enough for you to worry about estate taxes, insurance can be used to provide liquidity for your heirs to pay mortgages, debt payments, medical bills, and the like. This will go a long way to provide peace of mind and financial stability for your family.

Still More Trusts

A trust can be "created" for almost any situation, need, or goal imaginable. There are:

Spendthrift trusts
Discretionary distribution trusts
Accumulation trusts
IRS Code Sections 2503(b) and (c) trusts
Separate property trusts
Simple trusts

Complex trusts, etc.
There is even one called a crummy trust.

All of these "trusts" can be incorporated easily into a properly drawn revocable living trust. There is no need to reinvent the wheel for each minor or specific application you may have.

More People Now Benefit from Living Trusts

Once you understand the benefits of the living trust in your estate planning, you might ask, "If living trusts are so great, why aren't more people using them?" Increasing numbers are; however, most people are never informed as to their benefits. One of the main reasons is that except for estate planning attorneys who may advise clients of living trusts, many in the legal profession are more apt to suggest the use of wills; obviously, probate services are among the more lucrative aspects of a lawyer's work.

A gentleman recently stated that his lawyer advised him against a trust because his estate, valued at $500,000, was not large enough for him to need a trust to eliminate federal inheritance taxes.

Further inquiry revealed that the lawyer had not advised him about probate, which would amount to approximately 8 percent (the national average) of the estate, $40,000, to pay the lawyer's fees—in addition to

the other expenses. The lawyer never mentioned that his estate could be tied up for one or two years and that his family would lose control of the assets while the probate court "managed" his estate. That gentleman subsequently created a living trust.

Thus, lawyers often do not promote the living trust because they will lose probate fees. The probate department of a legal firm generates a substantial amount of income for that firm. In fact, many lawyers look upon wills as a type of annuity. File cabinets filled with wills are sources of enormous future income. The attorney's dilemma is between the client's best interests and his/her self-interest. Informed consumers should be allowed to make their own choices.

Anatomy of a Trust

Living trusts, unlike men, are *not* created equal, nor are they endowed with inalienable "rights." To be recognized as a valid estate planning device, the living trust document (or grantor trust, as it is referred to by the IRS) must be written to federal tax codes, specifically Section 676 et al., and regulations. Past this point, all equality between trusts ceases. The qualities of a living trust are determined as follows:

1. By the benefits and flexibility they afford the parties involved.

2. By the way management and distribution powers are built into the trusts.

A first-class revocable living trust should contain provisions that are *essential* if you are to retain full control of your trust estate. It should also provide your trustee(s) with real administrative power. In estate planning, *control* is the paramount objective.

Though revocable living trusts are an extremely valuable tool in estate planning, they may still be planned poorly or badly written.

The following document is an excellent example modeled on an existing type-A married revocable living trust document for a couple with children. Its provisions can provide for maximum managerial control over your trust assets and activities.

Should your planning require the use of an A-B or A-B-C (QTIP) revocable living trust, simply refer to the sections that specifically address those items.

Please note that the language pertaining to A-B and A-B-C trusts will be offset by brackets [   ]. Thus, if you do not have children, minor or adult, ignore those items that concern children. If you are single, remove all references to "spouse" and switch the plural tense to singular tense.

If you choose not to use one or more of the following items, *specifically exclude it*. For example, use the following language to accomplish this: "This provision not used." Later, it cannot be said that you forgot to include it in your trust document in order to call your intentions into question.

Married Living Trust A or [A-B] or [A-B-C]

DECLARATION OF A TRUST

You must declare for what purpose this trust is being created.

> **Declaration of Trust**
> This revocable Trust is formed to hold title to real and personal property for the benefit of the creators of this Trust and to provide for the orderly use and/or transfer of such assets upon their demise.

NAME OF THE TRUST

Select any name. The author's clients have named their trusts after their pets, grandchildren, ancestors, hometowns, streets, flowers, endangered species, initials, anagrams, acronyms, Greek islands, etc. One couple used their winning lottery number.

Typically, most use the family name.

The date on the trust is most important, as are the names of the trustors (persons granting the trust) and the trustees. These defining elements set your trust apart from any other trust that may have the same name, for example, the Jones Family Trust.

> This Trust shall be known as:
> The _____ Trust, dated _____, YOUR NAME
> and SPOUSE'S NAME, Trustors and/or Trustees.

PARTIES TO THE TRUST

Who are the people setting up the trust? What authority do they have? Where do they live? When creating a trust, use your real names.

> This Trust is entered into by and between YOUR NAME and SPOUSE'S NAME of the County of _____, State of _____, hereinafter called "Settlors" or "Trustors" or, separately, "Husband" or "Wife," and YOUR NAME and SPOUSE'S NAME of the County of _____, State of _____, hereinafter called "Trustees" or "Trustee," and "beneficiaries" or "beneficiary" while living.

TRUSTEE AUTHORITY TO ACT INDEPENDENTLY

Each spouse has the right to act independently as may be required and provide for a smooth change of power if the situation warrants. This power does not include sole and separate property situations (for example, if the husband owns property in his name and places it in the trust, the wife can perform any transaction in the trust except dispose of that property, which would require the husband's signature. The same is true if the wife is sole owner of property). In the event of the death of one spouse, then the surviving spouse may dispose of the husband's property as spelled out in the trust.

The above named Settlors and Trustees, YOUR NAME and SPOUSE'S NAME, shall serve jointly and severally and either shall have full authority for the Trust without the consent of the other, to act independently in performing transactions on behalf of the Trust. This authority shall extend to all powers granted to the Trustees under Trustee Powers hereof and shall include the right to contract for and in behalf of the Trust and to execute, negotiate, and compromise such instruments as may be necessary to carry out the purposes and intents of this Trust.

TAX TREATMENT OF REVOCABLE "GRANTOR TRUST"

It is absolutely necessary that your trust conform to IRS regulations as they apply to grantor trusts (grantor is the same as trustor or settlor).

Pursuant to "Settlor Powers" of this Trust, the Settlors have the right to amend this Trust in whole or in part and therefore, while the Settlors are alive, the Trust shall be treated as a revocable "Grantor Trust" for income tax purposes pursuant to the Internal Revenue Code Sec. 676. All items of income and expense related to the assets of the Trust or its operation shall be reported by the Settlors on the Settlors' tax returns, as required.

USE OF A TRUST IDENTIFICATION NUMBER

Apply for a trust identification number directly from the IRS, using form SS-4, the same form used to apply for an employer's ID number. Fill it in as per example below, and mail it back to the IRS. It will take about three weeks.

When you receive several items along with the number from the IRS, record this number, as specified below, and THROW EVERYTHING ELSE AWAY.

You will never use this ID number. As stated below, you will continue to use your own Social Security number(s) in all of your tax business.

As long as both husband and wife are living, this Trust is revocable. The Settlors shall use their individual Social Security Numbers as the Trust Identification Number—Social Security Number YOUR SOCIAL SECURITY NUMBER and SPOUSE'S SOCIAL SECURITY NUMBER. The Social Security Number of either Spouse is appropriate.

Upon the death of a Spouse, Trust A remains revocable and shall be identified by using the surviving Spouse's Social Security Number—SS No. _____. [Leave blank until death of first Spouse—author] Decedents' Trust B [and Decedents' Trust C] become irrevocable at the death of the first Spouse, and the assets in these Trusts shall be identified using an "Employer/ Trust Identification Number" assigned respectively to Trust B [and to Trust C].

[Identification Number, Trust B: _____.]
[Identification Number, Trust C: _____.]
[Enter IRS Trust Tax Identification Numbers when received.]

Upon the death of both husband and wife, the [entire] Trust becomes irrevocable by its terms, and assets retained in Trust should be identified by using an IRS Employer/Trust Identification Number _____. Enter IRS Trust Tax Identification Number when received. When [part, or all, of] the Trust becomes irrevocable, a Form 1041 tax return or appropriate alternative form, as specified by IRS regulations, shall be filed annually for the irrevocable part of the Trust.

Trust Property

Specify that the trust is intended to be the "owner" of all the assets in your estate. No inventory will be needed. In addition, you may state, if you desire, that any inheritance due you now or in the future shall be part of the trust.

Form SS-4 — Application for Employer Identification Number

Form SS-4
(Rev. August 1988)
Department of the Treasury
Internal Revenue Service

Application for Employer Identification Number

(For use by employers and others. Please read the attached instructions before completing this form.) Please type or print clearly.

Official Use Only

OMB No. 1545-0003
Expires 7-31-91

1 Name of applicant (True legal name. See instructions.)

NAME OF TRUST, Example: THE DOE FAMILY TRUST

2 Trade name of business if different from item 1

3 Executor, trustee, "care of name"
YOUR NAME(S)

4 Mailing address (street address) (room, apt., or suite no.)
YOUR MAILING ADDRESS

5 Address of business, if different from item 4. (See instructions.)

4a City, state, and ZIP code
YOUR CITY, STATE, ZIP

5a City, state, and ZIP code

6 County and State where principal business is located
YOUR COUNTY OF RESIDENCE

7 Name of principal officer, grantor, or general partner. (See instructions.) ▲ YOUR NAME(S)

8 Type of entity (Check only one.) (See instructions.)

- [ ] Individual SSN _____
- [ ] REMIC
- [ ] State/local government
- [ ] Other nonprofit organization (specify) _____
- [ ] Farmers' cooperative
- [ ] Estate
- [X] Other (specify) ▲ REVOCABLE ESTATE PLANNING TRUST— "GRANTOR"

- [ ] Personal service corp.
- [ ] National guard
- [ ] Trust

- [ ] Plan administrator SSN _____
- [ ] Other corporation (specify) _____
- [ ] Federal government/military
- [ ] Church or church controlled organization
  If nonprofit organization enter GEN (if applicable) _____
- [ ] Partnership

8a If a corporation, give name of foreign country (if applicable) or state in the U.S. where incorporated ▲
Foreign country _____   State _____

9 Reason for applying (check only one)

- [ ] Started new business
- [ ] Hired employees
- [ ] Created a pension plan (specify type) ▲ _____
- [ ] Banking purpose (specify) ▲ _____

- [ ] Changed type of organization (specify) ▲ _____
- [ ] Purchased going business
- [X] Created a trust (specify) ▲ GRANTOR TRUST
- [ ] Other (specify) ▲ _____

10 Business start date or acquisition date (Mo., day, year) (See instructions.)
DATE YOU SIGN LIVING TRUST DOCUMENT

11 Enter closing month of accounting year (See instructions.)
December

12 First date wages or annuities were paid or will be paid (Mo., day, year). **Note:** *If applicant is a withholding agent, enter date income will first be paid to nonresident alien. (Mo., day, year).* ▶ Not Applicable

13 Enter highest number of employees expected in the next 12 months. **Note:** *If the applicant does not expect to have any employees during the period, enter "0."*

| Nonagricultural | Agricultural | Household |
| -0- | -0- | -0- |

14 Does the applicant operate more than one place of business? . . . . ☐ Yes ☒ No
If "Yes," enter name of business. ▶

15 Principal activity or service (See instructions.) ▶ REVOCABLE GRANTOR ESTATE PLANNING TRUST

16 Is the principal business activity manufacturing? . . . . ☐ Yes ☒ No
If "Yes," principal product and raw material used. ▶

17 To whom are most of the products or services sold? Please check the appropriate box.
☐ Public (retail)   ☐ Other (specify) ▶   ☐ Business (wholesale)   ☒ N/A

18 Has the applicant ever applied for an identification number for this or any other business?. . . . . ☐ Yes ☒ No
Note: *If "Yes," please answer items 18a and 18b.*

18a If the answer to item 18 is "Yes," give applicant's true name and trade name, if different when applicant applied.

True name ▶   Trade name ▶

18b Enter approximate date, city, and state where the application was filed and the previous employer identification number if known.
Approximate date when filed (Mo., day, year)   City, and state where filed   Previous EIN

Under penalties of perjury, I declare that I have examined this application, and to the best of my knowledge and belief, it is true, correct, and complete.   Telephone number (include area code)

Name and title (please type or print clearly) ▶   PRINT YOUR NAME , Trustee   YOUR TELEPHONE NUMBER

Signature ▶   YOU SIGN HERE   Date ▶   DATE YOU SIGNED

Note: *Do not write below this line.*   For official use only.

Please leave blank ▶	Geo.	Ind	Class		Reason for applying

For Paperwork Reduction Act Notice, see Instructions.   ☆ U.S. Government Printing Office: 1988-523-133/00332   Form **SS-4** (Rev. 8-88)

Form SS-4

Application for Employer Identification Number

(Rev. August 1988)
Department of the Treasury
Internal Revenue Service

(For use by employers and others. Please read the attached instructions before completing this form.) Please type or print clearly.

Official Use Only

OMB No. 1545-0003
Expires 7-31-91

1 Name of applicant (True legal name. See instructions.)

2 Trade name of business if different from item 1

3 Executor, trustee, "care of name"

4 Mailing address (street address) (room, apt., or suite no.)

5 Address of business, if different from item 4. (See instructions.)

4a City, state, and ZIP code

5a City, state, and ZIP code

6 County and State where principal business is located

7 Name of principal officer, grantor, or general partner. (See instructions.) ▶

8 Type of entity (Check only one.) (See instructions.)

- ☐ Individual SSN : : :
- ☐ REMIC   ☐ Personal service corp.
- ☐ State/local government   ☐ National guard
- ☐ Other nonprofit organization (specify)
- ☐ Farmers' cooperative
- ☐ Estate   ☐ Trust
- ☒ Other (specify) ▶ REVOCABLE ESTATE PLANNING TRUST— "GRANTOR"

- ☐ Plan administrator SSN : : :
- ☐ Other corporation (specify)
- ☐ Federal government/military   ☐ Church or church controlled organization
- If nonprofit organization enter GEN (if applicable)
- ☐ Partnership

8a If a corporation, give name of foreign country (if applicable) or state in the U.S. where incorporated ▶   Foreign country   State

9 Reason for applying (check only one)

- ☐ Started new business
- ☐ Hired employees
- ☐ Created a pension plan (specify type) ▶
- ☐ Banking purpose (specify) ▶
- ☐ Changed type of organization (specify) ▶
- ☐ Purchased going business
- ☒ Created a trust (specify) ▶ GRANTOR TRUST
- ☐ Other (specify) ▶

10 Business start date or acquisition date (Mo., day, year) (See instructions.)

11 Enter closing month of accounting year (See instructions.)
December

12 First date wages or annuities were paid or will be paid (Mo., day, year). **Note:** If applicant is a withholding agent, enter date income will first be paid to nonresident alien. (Mo., day, year). ▸
Not Applicable

13 Enter highest number of employees expected in the next 12 months. **Note:** If the applicant does not expect to have any employees during the period, enter "0." ▸

Nonagricultural	Agricultural	Household
-0-	-0-	-0-

14 Does the applicant operate more than one place of business. ▸ ☐ Yes ☒ No
If "Yes," enter name of business. ▸

15 Principal activity or service (See instructions.) ▸ REVOCABLE GRANTOR ESTATE PLANNING TRUST

16 Is the principal business activity manufacturing?. ▸ ☐ Yes ☒ No
If "Yes," principal product and raw material used. ▸

17 To whom are most of the products or services sold? Please check the appropriate box. ☐ Business (wholesale)
☐ Public (retail) ☐ Other (specify) ▸ ☒ N/A

18 Has the applicant ever applied for an identification number for this or any other business?. ▸ ☐ Yes ☒ No
Note: If "Yes," please answer items 18a and 18b.

18a If the answer to item 18 is "Yes," give applicant's true name and trade name, if different when applicant applied.

True name ▸   Trade name ▸

18b Enter approximate date, city, and state where the application was filed and the previous employer identification number if known.

Approximate date when filed (Mo., day, year)	City, and state where filed	Previous EIN

Under penalties of perjury, I declare that I have examined this application, and to the best of my knowledge and belief, it is true, correct, and complete. | Telephone number (include area code)

Name and title (please type or print clearly) ▸ _____, Trustee

Signature ▸   Date ▸

Note: Do not write below this line. For official use only.

Please leave blank ▸	Geo.	Ind.	Class	Reason for applying

For Paperwork Reduction Act Notice, see instructions.

* U.S. Government Printing Office: 1988-523-133/00332

Form **SS-4** (Rev. 8-88)

The Trust is intended by the Trustors, YOUR NAME and SPOUSE'S NAME, to be the recipient of all their assets, whether jointly owned or separate, as well as the named beneficiary of all interests of which the Trustors are, or may become, beneficiaries.

PROPERTY TRANSFERRED TO THE TRUST

With this clause, you state that all property has, in fact, been transferred into your trust. Any items you may forget to transfer will be caught by the safety net of the pour over will.

The Settlors, YOUR NAME and SPOUSE'S NAME, have paid over, assigned, granted, conveyed, transferred and delivered, and by this Agreement do hereby pay over, assign, grant, convey, transfer and deliver unto the Trustee(s) their property and may cause the Trustee(s) to be designated as beneficiary of life insurance policies for and in behalf of the Trust and its beneficiaries. These insurance policies, and other insurance policies that may be delivered to the Trustee(s) hereunder or under which the Trustee may be designated as beneficiary, the proceeds of all such policies being payable to the Trustee(s), and any other property that may be received or which has been received by the Trustee(s) hereunder, as invested and reinvested (hereinafter referred to as the "trust estate"), shall be held, administered, and distributed by the Trustee(s) as hereinafter set forth.

COMMUNITY PROPERTY AND QUASI-COMMUNITY PROPERTY

In this section, you provide that the nature of assets transferred into your trust will not change because of this transfer. Quasi-community property pertains to jointly owned property in states other than community-property states.

Community and quasi-community property transferred to the Trustees by the Settlors shall be their community property. This property, as invested and reinvested, together with the rents, issues, and profits therefrom (herein referred to as the "community property") shall retain its character as community property during the joint lifetimes of the Settlors, in spite of any change in the situs of the Trust, subject, however, to the provisions of this Agreement.

SEPARATE PROPERTY

The same holds true for sole and separate property of either settlor. Its nature will not change due to any transfer to the trust as long as it is not commingled with jointly held assets.

Separate property of either Settlor transferred to the Trustee(s), as invested and reinvested, together with the rents, issues, and profits therefrom, hereinafter referred to as "the Separate Estate," shall retain its character as separate property of the Settlor who transferred such property to the Trustee(s), subject to the provisions of this Agreement.

Trustees

Provide for the passing or resignation of an original Trustee.

Upon the death, resignation, or incompetency of an original Trustee, the surviving or Successor Trustee becomes the manager of the Trust and its affairs.

SURVIVING TRUSTEE

Specify that if one of you should pass away, or become incompetent, or resign as trustee, the other is to serve as the remaining trustee.

In the event of the death of YOUR NAME, or if for any reason he ceases to serve as Trustee hereunder, the Trustors nominate and appoint SPOUSE'S NAME to serve as sole Trustee hereunder and without the approval of any court.

In the event of the death of SPOUSE'S NAME, or if for any reason she ceases to serve as Trustee hereunder, the Trustors nominate and appoint YOUR NAME to serve as sole Trustee hereunder and without the approval of any court.

SUCCESSOR TRUSTEE

You will appoint a successor trustee to take control upon the passing of both the husband and the wife. Should you appoint more than one successor trustee, then the second appointee(s) shall serve as either a co-trustee(s) or alternate trustee(s).

In the event of the death of the remaining or surviving original Trustee, YOUR NAME or SPOUSE'S NAME, or if for any reason such person ceases to serve as Trustee hereunder, the Trustors, YOUR NAME and SPOUSE'S NAME, nominate and appoint YOUR SUCCESSOR TRUSTEE to serve as Successor Trustee (co-trustees) hereunder without the approval of any court.

In the event of the death of the named Successor Trustee, or if for any reason the named

Successor Trustee ceases to serve as Trustee hereunder, the Trustors nominate and appoint YOUR ALTERNATE SUCCESSOR TRUSTEE(S) to serve as Successor Trustee (Co-trustees) hereunder without the approval of any court.

SUCCESSOR TRUSTEES MUST ACT TOGETHER

If you have appointed more than one successor trustee, provide that there be full and complete agreement in the management decisions made by the co-trustees.

When there is more than one Successor Trustee acting simultaneously with other designated Trustees, the Co-trustees so serving must act in concert. This provision does not apply to the Settlors.

When more than one person is named with others to act as Successor Co-trustees and one of the named persons is unable or unwilling for any reason to serve or to continue to serve, and no additional persons are named herein to take the place of such declining or retiring Trustee, the Settlors direct that the remaining named Successor Co-Trustee(s) shall continue to serve as Co-trustees (or if one only remains, Trustee) hereof without the approval of any court.

NO BOND REQUIREMENT

Since you will probably be naming one or more of your adult children or close family members as successor trustee(s), if you so choose, you may provide that they will not have to post a bond to serve in that capacity.

If you appoint a bank or other professional trustee service, you would definitely want them to be bonded. In that event, you change this clause to require that a bond be obtained.

> **No Trustee shall be required to post bond or any other security for the faithful performance of any duty or obligation of such office.**

RESOLUTION OF CONFLICT

One of the main reasons for setting up a revocable living trust is to avoid the pain, length of time, and expense of subjecting your estate to lawyers and the court system. Therefore, conflict between trustees and other parties should not be tolerated.

> **Any controversy between the Trustees and any other Trustee or Trustees, or between any other parties to this Trust, including beneficiaries, involving the construction or application of any of the terms, provisions, or conditions of this Trust shall, on the written request of either or any disagreeing party served on the other or others, be**

submitted to arbitration. Such arbitration shall comply with the commercial Arbitration Rules of the American Arbitration Association, 140 West 51st Street, New York, New York 10020. The decision of the arbitrator(s) shall be final and conclusive upon both parties. The cost of arbitration shall be borne by the losing party or in such proportion as the arbitrator(s) shall decide.

LITIGATION

The following clause speaks for itself. Heirs beware!

The Settlors, YOUR NAME and SPOUSE'S NAME, desire that this Trust, the trust estate, and the Trust administrators and beneficiaries shall not be involved in time-consuming and costly litigation concerning the function of this Trust and disbursement of the assets. Furthermore, the Settlors have taken great care to designate, through the provisions of this Trust, how they want the trust estate distributed. Therefore, if a beneficiary, or a representative of a beneficiary, or one claiming a beneficial interest in the trust estate, should legally challenge this Trust, its provisions, or asset distributions, then all asset distributions to said challenging beneficiary shall be retained in Trust and distributed to the remaining beneficiaries herein named, as if said challenging beneficiary and his or her issue had predeceased the distribution of the trust estate. The defense of such litigation, including costs incurred by representatives of the Settlor's estate, the Trustees of this Trust, and their agents, attorneys, accountants, and representatives, shall be paid for by the Trust.

DISCHARGE OR RESIGNATION OF TRUSTEE

You and your spouse have the right to change successor trustees at any time, and for any reason. You need not have cause for such an action.

Also, if a successor trustee so desires, he/she can resign that position.

The surviving Settlor shall have the right following the decedent Spouse's death to discharge the Trustee of any Trust hereunder including any Successor Trustee, and to appoint a Trustee in his/her place. Discharge of a Trustee shall be by delivery to such Trustee of thirty days' written notice of discharge.

The Trustee of any Trust hereunder, including any Successor Trustee, may resign by delivery to all the income beneficiaries of such Trust of thirty days' written notice of resignation. If no Successor Trustee is named by the Trust, such income beneficiaries who are adults shall have the right to appoint a Trustee, provided that if no such income beneficiaries are adults, then such appointment shall be made by the parent or legal guardian of such income beneficiaries; provided, further, that in the event of a dispute among such income beneficiaries, their parents or guardians, the majority shall prevail.

A discharged or resigned Trustee shall serve as Trustee until his/her successor shall accept office, and shall execute all instruments and do all acts necessary to vest title of the trust estate in the Successor Trustee without court accounting. However, any discharged Trustee shall have authority to apply to a court of competent jurisdiction to ensure that a Successor Trustee is appointed.

TRUSTEE COMPENSATION

If you choose to include this type of clause, you can provide that your successor trustee be compensated by the trust for time, effort, and expenses incurred in the management of the trust estate. Generally, annual professional administration fees range from .5 percent to 1 percent of the gross trust value of the trust estate, plus actual expenses.

The Trustee(s) shall be entitled to reasonable compensation for his or her services, which compensation shall be commensurate with comparable charges for similar services made from time to time by corporate Trustees in the geographic area in which the Trust has its principal situs for administration. The Trustee shall also be entitled to reimbursement for expenses necessarily incurred in the administration of the trust estate.

COMPETENCY CLAUSE

If you or your spouse is unable to administer the day-to-day affairs of the trust, you can ensure that control is retained by the family.

The Settlors, YOUR NAME and SPOUSE'S NAME, hereby provide that they may, by separate addenda to this agreement, designate two persons who shall be authorized and empowered to determine the competency of the appointing Settlor or Trustee of this agreement. The appointed persons shall be authorized and empowered to confirm in writing the incompetency or competency of the appointing Settlor, and their joint decision thereon shall be binding upon the Settlors, Trustees, and beneficiaries of this Trust.

If a Settlor has not named two persons of their choice by the separate addendum, or if one or both of the persons named are unable or unwilling to serve, the affected Settlor hereby authorizes their "Attorney-in-Fact" appointed under their Durable Power of Attorney for Health Care, if any, to name one or both doctors, as appropriate, to determine the competency of such Settlor in accordance with the foregoing provisions.

Confirmation of removal or reappointment of any Trustee removed for incompetency by reason of the determination of the appointed persons or whose competency to serve as Trustee hereunder has been re-certified by the appointed persons may be confirmed by application to a court of competent jurisdiction.

Settlor Powers

The trust provides the necessary powers for either settlor to retain the right to administer and deal in the trust property as they solely determine to be proper.

DESCRIPTION OF SETTLOR POWERS

The functions of the settlor in the living trust were described earlier. In this clause, those functions are further defined.

Both Settlors may, during the joint lives of the Settlors, by signed instruments delivered to the Trustee:

Withdraw the community estate from this Trust in any amount and at any time upon giving reasonable notice in writing to the Trustee and other Settlor, provided, however, that all or any part of the community estate withdrawn by the Settlors shall be delivered to the Settlors as community property;

Add community property to the Trust;

Change the beneficiaries, their respective shares and the plan of distribution;

Amend this Trust in any other respect; or

Revoke this Trust in its entirety or any provision therein; provided, however, the duties or responsibilities of a Trustee shall not be enlarged without a Trustee's consent nor without satisfactory adjustment of the Trustee's compensation.

Both Settlors are authorized and empowered with respect to any property, real or personal, to: assign, borrow, buy, care for, collect, compromise claims, contract with respect to, continue any business of a Settlor, convey, convert, deal with, dispose of, enter into, exchange, hold, improve, incorporate any business of a Settlor, invest, lease, manage, mortgage, hypothecate, encumber, grant and exercise options with respect to, take possession of, pledge, receive, release, repair, sell, sue for, make distributions in cash or in kind or partly in each without regard to the income tax basis of such asset, all for and in behalf of the Trust or for the Settlors' own accounts or to secure the Settlors' own debts or obligations or to guarantee the obligations of third parties.

SURVIVING SETTLOR RETAINS
ABSOLUTE RIGHT AS TRUSTEE

With this clause, you set up the mechanism whereby the surviving spouse retains the role as settlor and retains those powers associated with this position.

> After the death of one of the original Settlors, the surviving Settlor shall be the Trustee, unless and until, the Trustee resigns in writing, or is determined incompetent as per the terms herein provided. The surviving Settlor continues to retain all absolute rights to discharge or replace any Successor Trustee of any portion or share of the Trust which is revocable by the surviving Settlor, as long as the Settlor is competent.

Trustee(s)' Powers

As a trustee, you want as much power as possible granted to you via the trust document. Your intent is not to lose control but enhance it. As such, the clauses in this section are the cornerstone of your authority and control over "your" trust assets.

In addition, after your passing and that of your spouse, your successor trustee or co-trustees will need this same power base to actively manage the trust estate on behalf of the beneficiaries.

The Trustee(s) shall have the following powers, duties, and discretions in addition to those otherwise granted herein or by law, and expected as elsewhere herein specifically restricted.

JOINT TRUST PROPERTY

These clauses give to the trustee(s) powers over jointly owned property and benefit from same. You can place property into the trust, and you can remove property from the trust. If you remove property from the trust, it becomes "free of Trust," meaning that the provisions and protections of the trust no longer apply to that property.

The Trustee(s) shall have no more extensive power over any property transferred to the Trust than either Settlor would have under the property laws of the situs state, had this Trust not been created, and this instrument shall be so interpreted to achieve this intention.

The Trustee(s) shall hold, manage, invest, and reinvest the trust estate (if any requires such management and investment) and shall collect the income, if any, therefrom and shall dispose of the net income and principal during the joint lives of the Settlors as follows:

The Trustee(s) shall pay to, or apply for the benefit of the Settlors, as community property, all the net income of the community estate.

The Trustee(s) may pay to, or apply for the benefit of the Settlors, as community property, such sums from the principal of the trust estate as in its sole discretion shall be necessary or advisable from time to time for the medical care, welfare, and maintenance of the Settlors, taking into consideration to the extent the Trustee(s) deems/ deem advisable any other income or resources of the Settlors known to the Trustee(s).

Either Settlor may, at any time during the joint lives of the Settlors, and from time to time, withdraw all or any part of the principal of the trust estate, free of Trust, by delivering an instrument in writing, duly signed by him or her, to the Trustee and to the other Settlor, describing the property or portion thereof desired to be withdrawn. Upon receipt of such instrument, the Trustee(s) shall thereupon convey and deliver to the Settlors, as community property, free of Trust, the property described in such instrument.

SEPARATE PROPERTY

Just as in the previous clauses concerning jointly held assets, the same holds true for separately held assets. If you choose, you can commingle these assets, and thereby change their nature to that of community or quasi-community property.

The Trustee(s) shall hold, manage, invest, and reinvest the separate estate of each Settlor (if any requires such management and investment) and shall collect the income, if any, therefrom and shall dispose of the net income and principal during the joint lives of the Settlors as follows:

The Trustee(s) shall pay to, or apply for the benefit of the Settlor who contributed such separate estate, all of the net income of such Settlor's separate estate.

The Trustee(s) may pay to, or apply for the benefit of the Settlor who contributed such separate estate, such sums from the principal thereof as in its sole discretion shall be necessary or advisable from time to time for the medical care, welfare, and comfortable maintenance of such Settlor, taking into consideration to the extent the Trustee(s) deems/deem advisable, any other income and resources of such Settlor known to the Trustee(s).

The Settlor who contributed such separate estate may at any time, during the joint lives of the Settlors and from time to time, withdraw all or any part of the principal of such separate estate, free of Trust, by delivering an instrument in writing duly signed by him or her to the Trustee(s), describing the property or portion thereof desired to be withdrawn. Upon receipt of such instrument, the Trustee(s) shall thereupon convey and deliver to such Settlor, as his or her separate property, free of Trust, the property described in such instrument.

RETENTION

This section allows the trust to hold any type of asset, whether specifically mentioned or not. It also gives you the power to manage said assets and operate a business from within the trust itself.

The Trustee(s) shall have the power to retain, without liability for loss or depreciation resulting from such retention, the original assets and all other property hereafter transferred, devised, or bequeathed to the Trustee(s), although such property may not be of the character prescribed by law or by the terms of this instrument for the investment of other Trust assets; and, although it represents a large percentage or all of the trust estate, this said original property may accordingly be held as a permanent investment.

The Trustee(s) shall have the power, with respect to any business interest that may become a part of the trust estate, whether organized as a sole proprietorship, partnership, or corporation, and upon such terms for such time and in such manner as it may deem advisable, to hold, retain, and continue to operate such business solely at the risk of the trust estate and without liability on the part of the Trustee(s) for any losses resulting therefrom; to dissolve, liquidate, or sell at such time and upon such terms as the Trustee(s) may deem advisable; to incorporate such business and hold the stock as an asset of the trust estate; to use the general assets of the Trust for the purpose of the business; to borrow money for business purposes and pledge or encumber the assets of the business or the other assets of the trust estate to secure the loan; to employ such officers, managers, employees, or agents as it may deem advisable in the management of such business, including electing directors, officers, or employees of the Trustee(s) to take part in the management of such business as directors or officers.

GENERAL PROPERTY POWERS

The following clauses provide an extensive range of power and latitude of judgment on the part of the trustee(s).

The Trustee(s) shall have all such powers and is/are authorized to do all such acts, take all such proceedings, and exercise all such rights and privileges in the management of the trust estate as if the absolute owner thereof, including, without limiting the generality of the terms, the right to manage, control, sell, convey, exchange, partition, assign, divide, subdivide, improve, or repair; to grant options and to sell upon deferred payments; to lease for terms within or extending beyond the duration of the Trust concerned for any purpose, including the exploration for and removal of oil, gas, and other minerals; to enter into community oil leases, pooling and unitization agreement; to create restrictions, easements, and other servitudes; to compromise, arbitrate, or otherwise adjust claims in favor of or against the Trust; to institute, compromise, and defend actions and proceedings at the expense of the trust estate; and to carry such insurance as the Trustee(s) may deem advisable.

POWER REGARDING SECURITIES

Brokerage houses require the following powers, provided in your trust document, should you wish to invest or trade securities.

The Trustee(s) shall have, respecting securities, all the rights, powers, and privileges of an owner, including the right to vote stock, give proxies, pay assessments and other sums deemed by the Trustee(s) to be necessary for the protection of the trust estate; to participate in voting Trusts, pooling agreements, foreclosures, reorganizations, consolidations, mergers and liquidations, and, in connection therewith, to deposit securities with and transfer title to any protective or other committee under such terms as the Trustee(s) may deem advisable; to exercise or sell stock subscription or conversion rights; to open an account with a brokerage firm of the choosing of the Trustee(s) in the Trustee's name, in its own behalf for the purpose of purchasing and selling of all kinds of securities and authorizing such brokerage firm to act upon any orders, including margin orders, options, both covered and uncovered, instructions with respect to such accounts and/or the delivery of securities or money therefrom and received from said Trustee(s); and to retain as an investment any securities or other property received through the exercise of any of the foregoing powers. The Trustee(s) is further authorized to sign, deliver, and/or receive any documents necessary to carry out the powers contained within this paragraph.

EXERCISE STOCK OPTIONS

Even if you never "play the market," you may still want to give yourself the right to do so.

The Trustee(s) is expressly authorized in the Trustee's sole discretion to exercise any option to purchase stock under any stock option purchase plan in which a beneficiary is a participant or may hold such option rights to the extent that any such option rights may be exercised by the Trustee(s) even though the stock involved is stock of a corporation which may be serving as corporate Trustee(s) hereunder, regardless of the amount of such stock or the percentage of the trust estate which may be invested in such stock before or after any purchase under such option.

INVESTMENT POWERS

With a fully contingent, revocable living trust, you will be able to maintain the same degree of control as you have now. (Contingent refers to having a trust document that will be applicable to all possible management abilities and situations.)

General

The Trustee(s) has the power to invest and reinvest principal and income, to purchase or acquire therewith every kind of property, real, personal, or mixed, and every kind of investment, specifically including, but not by way of limitation, shares in one or more mutual funds, in any common trust funds administered by the Trustee(s), corporate obligations of every kind, and stock, preferred or common, which persons of prudence and discretion and intelligence acquire for their own accounts.

The Trustee(s) is/are further authorized to buy, sell, and trade in securities of any nature (including short sales) on margin, and for such purposes may maintain and operate margin accounts with brokers, and may pledge any securities held or purchased by them with such brokers as security for loans and advances made to the Trustee(s).

Life Insurance and Annuities

The Trustee(s) is/are authorized in the Trustee's discretion to maintain and/or purchase policies of life insurance and/or annuities on the

104

life or for the benefit of any Trust beneficiaries and to hold and pay for the same as an investment and asset of the Trustee(s), at any time and upon successive occasions, the premiums to be charged against income or principal, as the Trustee(s) shall determine.

The Trustee(s) shall have the following powers, duties, and discretions with respect to policies of life insurance held as a part of the trust estate:

The Trustee(s) may pay premiums, assessments, or other charges with respect to such policies together with all other charges upon such policies or otherwise required to preserve them as binding contracts, but shall be under no duty to do so.

In the event that the Trustee(s) intends/intend not to pay any premium, assessment, or other charge with respect to any policy held by it, or otherwise intends to cancel, convert, or substantially modify any such policy, it shall first give the insured, or the guardian of the person of an insured under disability, at least fifteen (15) days' advance written notice of its intention to take such action.

Any amounts received by the Trustee(s) with respect to any policy as a dividend shall be treated as principal.

Upon the receipt of proof of death of any person whose life is insured for the benefit of any Trust hereunder, or upon maturity of any policy payable to the Trustee(s) prior to the death of the insured, the Trustee(s) shall collect all sums payable with respect thereto and shall thereafter hold such sums as principal of the respective trust estate, except that any interest paid by the insurer for a period subsequent to maturity shall be considered as income.

The Trustee(s) may accept any payments due it under any settlement arrangement made before or after the death of the insured and may exercise any rights available to it under such arrangement.

The Trustee(s) may compromise, arbitrate, or otherwise adjust claims upon any policies, and may, but shall not be required to, exercise any settlement options available under such policies. The receipt of the Trustee(s) to the insurer shall be a full discharge and the insurer is not required to see to the application of the proceeds.

DETERMINATION OF INCOME AND PRINCIPAL

As trustee, you control income generated by trust assets and how those funds are to be spent. When income taxes are due, you will simply file the appropriate schedule with your federal 1040 return and, where applicable, your state income tax form.

The Trustee(s) shall have the power and the authority to determine income and principal, and show receipts and disbursements, including the fees of the Trustee(s), which shall be credited, charged, or apportioned as between income and principal; however, all such determination shall be made in accordance with the law of the state of the situs of the Trust and the decision and the accounts of the Trustee(s) in accordance with said provisions shall be binding on all persons in interest.

Notwithstanding the foregoing, the Trustee(s) shall: (1) allocate to principal all dividends or other payments made by any corporation or mutual investment company that is designated by the company as distribution of capital gains; (2) where a premium has been paid or a discount received in connection with the purchase of a bond, amortize such premium or discount by making an appropriate charge or credit to income, as the case may be; and (3) charge income from time to time with a reasonable reserve for (a) depreciation of all income-producing depreciable real or personal property, and capital improvements and extraordinary repairs on income-producing property; (b) depletion of all depletable natural resources; and (c) all intangible property having a limited economic life. Such allocations and charges need not be made, however, if written consents are obtained from all income beneficiaries and remaindermen, vested or contingent, living and competent to act. [A remainderman is anyone who would have a future beneficial interest in the assets of a trust.]

AUTHORITY TO BORROW AND ENCUMBER

You can loan *to* and loan *from* your trust, and use trust assets as collateral and security for said loans.

The Trustee(s) shall have the power to borrow money for any Trust purpose upon such terms and conditions as the Trustee(s) may deem proper, and to obligate the trust estate for repayment and to encumber the trust estate or any of its property by mortgage, deed of Trust, pledge or otherwise, using such procedure to consummate the transaction as the Trustee(s) may deem advisable.

In addition to the power to encumber property for a loan being made to the Trust, the Trustee(s) is/are specifically authorized and empowered to obligate, hypothecate, and encumber the trust estate by mortgage, deed of Trust, pledge or otherwise, or whatever form the Trustee(s) deem(s) appropriate, or to act as a third party guarantor to guarantee private borrowings of the Trustors or either of them during their joint lifetime. Upon the death of a Settlor, such guarantee may only be made from the Survivor's Trust A.

Loans to Trust

The Trustee(s) shall have the power to, in the Trustee's discretion, advance funds to any Trust herein created for any Trust purpose, such advances with interest at current rates to be a first lien on and be paid out of the principal and as expense of the Trust; and to reimburse the Trustee(s) from principal or accumulated income for any loss or expense incurred by reason of a Trustee's ownership or holding of any property in this Trust.

To Beneficiaries

The Trustee(s) may, at any time and upon successive occasions, loan such sums to the beneficiaries or any of them as the Trustee(s) shall deem advisable and in the best interest of the beneficiaries, such loan or loans, if made, to bear interest at the prevailing rate and to be unsecured or secured, as the Trustee(s) may, in the Trustee's discretion, direct, provided, however, that the Trustee(s) shall have wide discretion in making or denial of any such loan, and the Trustee's judgment in the matter shall be conclusive and binding on any beneficiary requesting any such loan.

DISTRIBUTIONS TO OR FOR MINOR OR INCOMPETENT

You can control how the distribution to a minor or incompetent is to be made.

If at any time any beneficiary entitled to receive income and/or principal hereunder shall be a minor or an incompetent or a person whom the Trustee(s) deem(s) to be unable, wisely or properly, to handle funds if paid to him or her directly, the Trustee(s) may make any such payments, in the Trustee's discretion, in any one or more, or any combination, of the following ways:

Directly to such beneficiary, or

To the natural guardian or the legally appointed guardian, conservator or other fiduciary of the person or estate of such beneficiary, or

To any person or organization furnishing support for such beneficiary, or by the Trustee(s) retaining the principal and making expenditures directly for the support of such beneficiary.

The Trustee(s) shall not be required to see to the application of any funds so paid or applied, and the receipt of such payee if disbursed for such purpose in the best judgment of the Trustee(s) shall be full acquittance to the Trustee(s). The decision of the Trustee(s) as to direct payments or application of funds in the manner herein prescribed shall be conclusive and binding upon all parties in interest if made in good faith. The Trustee(s) is/are requested to make all such disbursements in a way calculated to dispense with the necessity of guardianship proceedings.

The Trustee(s) may, in its sole and absolute discretion, require such reports and take such steps as it may deem requisite to assure and enforce the due application of such money to the purposes aforesaid.

DISBURSEMENT FOR FUNERAL
AND LAST ILLNESS

Should one of your beneficiaries predecease you, the authority to pay for his or her last illness and funeral expenses is given with this clause.

> The Trustee(s) may pay for the last illness, funeral and burial expenses of either Trustor or of any other beneficiary of this Trust unless adequate provision shall have been made, therefore, through his or her probate estate or otherwise.

NOTIFICATION OF TRUSTEE

Should the life course or situation of one or more of your beneficiaries change, you can not be held liable if no changes were made in your document that reflected this new potential allocation or situation. For example, you have allocated 5 percent to each grandchild named. If one of your children has a child that you are not aware of, that child would not be included automatically in this distribution.

> Until the Trustee(s) shall receive written notice of any birth, marriage, death, or other event upon which the right to payment from this Trust may depend, the Trustee(s) shall incur no liability for disbursements or distributions made or omitted in good faith.

DIVISION OF TRUSTS

You and your spouse, and your successor trustee(s) after you, have the power to determine asset values and division thereof for the purposes of distribution.

In making the distributions to any Trust or share created under this Agreement, the judgment of the Trustee(s) concerning the valuation of assets distributed shall be binding and conclusive upon all beneficiaries. The Trustee(s) may distribute the shares to the various Trusts or to beneficiaries by making distribution in cash, or in kind, or partly in cash and partly in kind, or in undivided interest, in such manner as the Trustee(s), in its sole and absolute discretion, deems advisable. The Trustee(s) may sell such property as it deems necessary to make any such division or distribution. The Trustee(s) shall not be required to make physical division of the Trust property, except when necessary for the purposes of distribution, but may, in the Trustee's discretion, maintain and keep the assets of any separate Trusts in one or more consolidated Trust funds, and as to each consolidated Trust fund, the division into various shares comprising such Trust fund need to be made only upon the Trustee's books of account, in which each separate Trust shall be allotted its proportional share of the principal and income of the consolidated fund and shall be charged with its proportionate part of expenses thereof.

PROVISIONS FOR TAXES

In this clause, you, and subsequently your trust estate after your passing, are empowered to pay any and all type of taxes that may be due. With an A-type single, A married, or A-B married living trust, those taxes will be due within nine months after your death or that of the *first* spouse. Under an A-B-C trust, those taxes are due within nine months after the passing of the *surviving* spouse.

If the trust estate has insufficient funds on hand to pay those taxes, a beneficiary can pay them and the trust can reimburse that beneficiary.

A better solution might be to use insurance proceeds to pay those taxes, thereby providing your estate with needed liquidity.

Upon the death of either Trustor, YOUR NAME or SPOUSE'S NAME, or of any other beneficiary, any estate, inheritance, succession or other death taxes, duties, charges or assessments, together with interest, penalties, costs, Trustee's compensation and attorney's fees, which shall become due by reason of the trust estate or any interest therein being includable in the Estate of either Trustor, or of such other beneficiary, for such tax purposes, may be paid from the trust estate by the Trustee(s), in its sole discretion, unless other adequate provision shall have been made therefore. Any such payments shall be charged to the principal of the trust estate. The Trustee(s) may make such payments directly, or to the Executory or other fiduciary of the Trustors or such other beneficiary, and may rely upon the written statement of such fiduciary as to the amount and propriety of such taxes, interest, penalties, and other costs. The decision of the Trustee(s) as to any such payments shall be conclusive and binding upon all parties interested in this Trust or such Estate. If the trust estate shall be then insufficient or if it be then terminated the Trustee(s) shall be reimbursed by the persons to whom the trust estate shall have been distributed, to the extent of the amount received by each distributee. The Trustee(s), before making any distribution of either income or principal, may accordingly require a refunding agreement or may withhold distribution pending determination or release of any tax lien.

The Trustee(s) is/are authorized to acquire by purchase, exchange or otherwise, property, real, personal, or mixed, from the Executor or Administrator of the Estate of any beneficiary of this Trust, even though such property may not be of a character prescribed by law or by the terms of the Trust instrument for the investment of Trust funds, and although the acquisition of such property may result in a large percentage or all of the trust estate being invested in one class of property. The Trustee(s) is expressly authorized to retain the property so acquired so long as it shall deem this advisable and to make secured or unsecured loans to the Executor or administrator of such Estate upon such terms as the Trustee(s) shall deem advisable, such procedures being authorized to the extent that they do not adversely affect or diminish the marital deduction available to the Estate. Such purchases or loans shall be without liability to the Trustee(s) for loss resulting to the trust estate therefrom. In any dealings with a fiduciary of the Estate, the Trustee(s) may rely upon the statement of such fiduciary as to all material facts.

Any portion of the trust estate which was received from any qualified plan as described in Section 2039 of the Internal Revenue Code of 1954, as amended, or any subsequent like or similar law, may not be used for any purpose described in this Article, which would result in the inclusion of said funds in the taxable Federal Estate of the Trustor so long as other sources of funds are available.

If the Trustee(s) considers/consider that any distribution from a Trust hereunder other than pursuant to a power to withdraw or appoint is a taxable distribution subject to a generation-skipping tax payable by the distributee, the Trustee(s) shall augment the distribution by an amount which the Trustee(s) estimates/estimate to be sufficient to pay the tax and shall charge the same against the Trust to which the tax relates. If the Trustee(s) considers that any termination of an interest in or power over Trust property hereunder is a taxable termination subject to a generation-skipping tax, the Trustee(s) shall pay the tax from the Trust property to which the tax relates, without adjustment of the relative inter-ests of the beneficiaries. If the tax is imposed in part by reason of the Trust property hereunder and in part by reason of other property, the Trustee(s) shall pay that portion thereof which the value of the Trust property bears to the total property taxed, taking into consideration deduc-tions, exemptions, and other factors which the Trustee(s) deem(s) pertinent.

PAYMENT OF TRUST EXPENSES

As herein provided, your trust estate has the power to pay any and all bills and expenses associated with the management of your estate.

The Trustee(s) shall have the authority to pay all costs, charges, and expenses of the trust es-tate, together with reasonable compensation for the Trustee's services hereunder, including ser-vices in whole or partial distribution of the trust estate; and to employ and compensate from the trust estate such agents, assistants, and attorneys as in the Trustee's judgment shall be necessary to protect and manage the Trust property.

USE OF HOME

In this clause, you give yourself, and any of your bene-ficiaries, the right to live in your own home. This may seem a little silly, but remember that you must give your trust all of the same rights and privileges you enjoy now. Don't provide power by assumption. Spell it all out.

The Trustee(s) shall allow the Settlors, YOUR NAME and SPOUSE'S NAME, to occupy and use until their deaths the home (or any interest therein) used by either or both Settlors as a principal residence. The Trustee(s) shall, at the discretion of the surviving Settlor, sell such home and, if such Survivor so directs, purchase and/or build another comparable residence to be used as a home for the surviving Settlor, and so on from time to time. The surviving Settlor shall not be required to pay any rent for the use of any such home.

On the death of the Survivor, in the discretion of the Co-trustee(s) or Successor Trustee(s), the home (or any interest therein) used by either or both Trustors as a principal residence at the time of the death of the Survivor may be retained by the Trustee for use as a residence by the minor children of either Trustor. The provisions of this paragraph shall apply notwithstanding that an interest in such home may be held by a Trust for the benefit of a beneficiary not residing in such home and notwithstanding the fact that a child having such residency is not a beneficiary of a then existing Trust.

Subject to the foregoing occupancies, any such home (or interest therein) held by the Trustee(s), or the proceeds from the sale thereof, shall be part of the principal of this/these Trust(s). All taxes, insurance, repairs, and assessments concerning such home shall, in the discretion of the Trustee(s), be paid out of the trust estate containing such home.

COMMENCE OR DEFEND LITIGATION

This gives you and your trust the power to defend yourselves against legal attack.

The Trustee(s) may commence or defend such litigation with respect to the Trust or any property of the trust estate as the Trustee(s) may deem advisable at the expense of the Trust.

COMPROMISE CLAIMS

This gives you and your trust the power to negotiate on behalf of the trust.

The Trustee(s) may compromise or otherwise adjust any claims or litigation against or in favor of the Trust.

ADJUST FOR TAX CONSEQUENCES

This clause provides the power to manage the entire trust estate in a manner that will minimize any tax consequence and liability.

The Trustee(s) shall have the power, in the Trustee's absolute discretion, to take any action and to make any election to minimize the tax liabilities of this Trust and its beneficiaries and to allocate the benefits among the various beneficiaries and to make adjustments in the rights of any beneficiaries or between the income and the principal accounts, to compensate for the consequence of any tax election or any investment or administrative decision that the Trustee(s) believes has had the effect of directly or indirectly preferring one beneficiary or group of beneficiaries over others.

BUDGET INCOME AND EXPENSES

You have the right to manage any and all income, and this right is transferred to your surviving spouse and successor trustee(s).

The Trustee(s) shall have the power to budget the estimated annual income and expenses of the Trust or Trust share in such manner as to equalize as far as possible periodic income payments to beneficiaries.

Payment of Death Costs

This section of your trust document provides for the payment of appropriate expenditures related to your passing as well as your spouse's.

The Trustee(s) shall pay the death costs of a decedent Settlor, YOUR NAME and SPOUSE'S NAME, as the Trustee deems most appropriate.

DISCRETIONARY POWERS OF TRUSTEE(S)

This clause provides the type and nature of expenses your trust estate can incur and what bills it can pay.

After a Settlor's death, the Trustee(s) may, with discretion, pay all or any part of a deceased Settlor's funeral and last illness expenses, legally enforceable claims against the Settlor or his or her estate, reasonable expenses of administration of his or her estate, any allowances by court order to those dependent upon such Settlor, any estate, inheritance, succession, death or similar taxes payable by reason of such Settlor's death, together with any interest thereon or other additions thereto, without reimbursement from any person. All such payments, except for interest, shall be charged generally against the principal of the trust estate includable in such Settlor's

> estate for Federal estate tax purposes and any interest so paid shall be charged generally against the income thereof.

WRITTEN STATEMENT AS EVIDENCE

The following clause can be used to simplify trust estate accounting.

> Written statement by the executor(s) or administrator(s) of debts, obligations, or expenses payable by the estate of a decedent shall be sufficient evidence of their amount and propriety for the protection of the Trustee(s), Co-trustee(s), or Successor Trustee(s) and the Trustee(s) shall be under no duty to see to the application of any such payments.

Death of Settlor

Upon the passing of either spouse or both, your trust may divide into shares if it is an A-B or A-B-C trust. If the value of the estate is less than the amount at which a division would benefit the estate, the surviving spouse or successor trustee(s) may elect not to divide the estate.

If you have a dividable trust, use the language found in number 2 to provide for this division. If you have a simple A-type married or single revocable living trust, use the language in number 1.

> **1.** Upon or after the death of a Settlor, the Trustee(s) shall hold, administer, and distribute the trust estate as follows:
>
> **2.** [Upon the death of either Settlor, the Trustee(s) shall divide the trust estate into two (2) separate shares. Such division shall include any property which may be added from the deceased Settlor's general estate. One share shall be designated as Survivor's Trust A and the other share shall be designated as [Decedent's Marital Share,] Trust B [and Trust C].

SURVIVOR'S TRUST A

Trust A holds one-half of all the jointly owned property plus any separate property of the surviving spouse. Use this model clause if you will be setting up a dividable A-B or A-B-C trust. Ignore it if your trust is an A-type married or A single trust.

> [Survivor's Trust A shall consist of one-half (½) interest in the community property of the trust estate, and the Separate Property of the surviving Settlor. Upon creation of this Trust, Survivor's Trust A shall remain revocable during the life of the surviving Settlor. Upon the death of the surviving Settlor, this share shall become irrevocable.]

122

DECEDENT'S MARITAL SHARE

This clause provides for taxes. Use this model clause if you will be setting up a dividable A-B or A-B-C trust. Ignore it if your trust is an A-type married or A single trust.

[Decedent's Marital Share shall consist of one-half (½) interest in the community property of the trust estate, one-half (½) interest in the quasi-community property of the trust estate, and all of the separate property of the Decedent Settlor. Decedent's Marital Share shall be placed into Decedent's Trust B [and Trust C]. Upon creation of such Trust shares, Decedent's Trust B [and Trust C] is/are irrevocable.

The Trustee(s) shall have the sole discretion to select that portion of the joint community assets which shall be included in the Marital Share (Decedent's Trust B [and Trust C]). [In no event, however, shall there be included in Trust C any assets or the proceeds of any asset which will not qualify for the federal estate tax marital deduction, and Trust C shall be reduced to the extent that it cannot be created with such qualifying assets.] The Trustee(s) shall value any asset selected by the Trustee(s) for distribution in kind to the Marital Share at the value of such asset at the date of distribution to the Marital Share.]

MAXIMUM MARITAL DEDUCTION

Use this model clause if you will be setting up a dividable A-B or A-B-C trust. Ignore it if your trust is an A married or A single trust.

[The term "maximum marital deduction" shall not be construed as a direction by the deceased Settlor to exercise any election respecting the deduction of estate administration expenses, the determination of the estate tax valuation date, or any other tax election which may be available under any tax laws. It is the intent of the Settlors that the maximum trust estate be available for the support of the surviving Settlor, whether in Trust A, [Trust B,] [or Trust C] and therefore the Settlors desire that no (or a minimum estate tax) be paid at the death of the first of the Settlors to die, and that the maximum marital deduction be used for this purpose, as appropriate.]

DIVISION OF MARITAL SHARE

Use this model clause if you will be setting up a dividable A-B or A-B-C trust. Ignore it if your trust is an A-type married or A single trust.

[The Marital Share shall be divided and administered as follows: An amount equal to the equivalent exemption available by reason of the unified tax credit available under Internal Revenue Code Section 2010 or any successor or modified version of that Section and shall be administered under the terms of Trust B as hereinafter set forth (Decedent's Trust B) and any amount of the Marital Share exceeding the amount allocated to Trust B shall be administered under the terms of Trust A [Trust C] as hereinafter set forth.]

DECEDENT'S TRUST B

Trust B holds one-half of all the jointly owned property plus any separate property of the decedent spouse. This amount should not exceed the current personal estate exemption of $600,000. Assets of the decedent spouse in excess of the above amount will flow into Trust C. Use this model clause if you will be setting up a dividable A-B or A-B-C trust. Ignore it if your trust is an A married or A single trust.

[Decedent's Trust B shall be composed of cash, securities, or other property of the trust estate (undiminished by any estate, inheritance, succession, death, or similar taxes) having a value equal to the largest amount, that after allowing for the unified credit against the federal estate tax and the state death tax credit against such tax (but only to the extent that the use of such state death tax credit does not increase the death tax payable to any state) will not result in a federal estate tax being imposed on the estate of the deceased Settlor.]

DECEDENT'S TRUST C

This trust holds the balance of the value of the trust estate over and above the $600,000 placed in the decedent's Trust B and the one-half of the estate's value placed in the survivor's Trust A. Taxes will be due on what *remains* in this Trust C upon the passing of the surviving spouse, not what went into it initially. Use this model clause if you will be setting up a dividable A-B-C trust. Ignore it if your trust is an A married, A single, or A-B trust.

[Trust C shall be composed of cash, securities, or other property of the trust estate (undiminished by any estate, inheritance, succession, death, or similar taxes) having a value equal to the maximum marital deduction as finally determined in the predeceased Spouse's federal estate tax proceedings, less the aggregate amount of marital deductions, if any, allowed for such estate tax purposes by reason of property or interest in property, passing or which have passed to the surviving Spouse, otherwise than pursuant to the provisions of this article, reduced by the amount of cash, securities, or other property allocated to Trust B herein.]

ELECTION OF FISCAL YEAR

This allows you to choose a different fiscal year for the trust if it would be beneficial. Use this model clause if you will be setting up a dividable A-B or A-B-C trust. Ignore it if your trust is an A married or A single living trust.

[The Trustee(s) may elect a different fiscal year for Decedent's Trust B [and C].]

USE OF TRUST B—SIMULTANEOUS DEATH

This can minimize tax liabilities to the estate. Use this model clause if you will be setting up a dividable A-B or A-B-C trust. Ignore it if your trust is an A married or A single trust.

[If both Settlors shall die simultaneously, the community property of the trust estate shall be divided equally between Trust A and Trust B. The Trustee(s) shall designate one of the Trust shares so created for each of the Settlors and shall allocate the separate property of each Settlor to their respective Trust shares. Each Trust, A and B, so created shall be separately held and administered by the Trustee(s) in accordance with the provisions and dispositions of the Trust on the demise of the surviving Settlor as herein defined.]

Survivor's Trust A

The following clauses—Right to Income, Right to Principal, Right to Withdraw Principal, Control of Assets, Right to Change Beneficiary, and Distribution of Residual of Trust A—set forth the rights afforded the surviving spouse under the survivor's Trust A section of an A married, A-B, or A-B-C revocable living trust.

> Upon or after the death of a Settlor, the Trustee(s) shall hold, administer, and distribute the trust estate as follows:

RIGHT TO INCOME

The survivor's Trust A holds the assets allocated to the surviving spouse. These assets "belong" to the surviving spouse, who has absolute control over those assets placed into this trust division.

> Commencing with the date of predeceased Spouse's death, the Trustee(s) shall pay to or apply for the benefit of the surviving Spouse, during his or her lifetime, all the net income from the trust estate in convenient installments but no less frequently than quarterly.

RIGHT TO PRINCIPAL

Since the assets are under complete control of the surviving spouse, he/she has the right to spend the trust estate on whatever he/she desires. The surviving spouse may even spend the entire amount of these funds.

In addition, the Trustee(s) may pay to or apply for the benefit of the surviving Spouse such sums from the principal of Trust A as in their sole discretion shall be necessary or advisable from time to time for the medical care, comfortable maintenance, and welfare of the surviving Spouse, taking into consideration to the extent the Trustee(s) deem(s) advisable any other income or resources of the surviving Spouse known to the Trustee(s).

RIGHT TO WITHDRAW PRINCIPAL

The surviving spouse may remove all of the assets in Trust A if said spouse wishes. This would effectively "de-fund" the trust and remove the protection afforded to those assets by the trust. As long as the surviving spouse is the trustee of Trust A, no written notice is needed to execute any action that affects the assets held in the trust estate.

The surviving Spouse may, at any time during his or her lifetime and from time to time, withdraw all or any part of the principal of the trust estate, free of Trust, by delivering to the Trustee(s) an instrument in writing, duly signed by the surviving Spouse, describing the property or portion thereof desired to be withdrawn. Upon receipt of such instrument, the Trustee(s) shall thereupon convey and deliver to the surviving Spouse, free of Trust, the property described in such instrument.

CONTROL OF ASSETS

The surviving spouse has the same control over the assets in the trust as if he/she "owned" those assets in their individual name. He/she may make any investment decision free of encumbrance by other parties. Again, as long as the surviving spouse is the trustee of Trust A, no written notice is needed.

The surviving Spouse may, at any time by written notice, require the Trustee(s) either to make any nonproductive property of this Trust productive or to convert productive property to nonproductive property, each within a reasonable time. The surviving Spouse may further require the Trustee(s) to invest part, or all, of this share of Trust assets for the purpose of maximizing income rather than growth, or growth rather than income.

RIGHT TO CHANGE BENEFICIARY

Under the provisions of an A-type married revocable living trust, the surviving spouse, if that person is the trustee, retains the right to remove or add beneficiaries as he or she wishes. Even after the passing of the first spouse, Trust A remains revocable, and therefore changeable by the surviving spouse.

> The surviving Spouse retains the right to change the beneficiaries of this Trust.

DISTRIBUTION OF RESIDUAL OF TRUST A

The surviving spouse can change the allocation and distribution to the beneficiaries of the trust. This means that while he or she is the trustee of the trust, changes can be made that impact upon who is an heir, what they are to receive, and when they are to receive their share or specific asset(s).

You, as an original trustee, have the absolute right to spend every last dime on whatever and however you choose. The trust is for your benefit while you are living. Residual distribution means exactly that. The successor trustee(s) is going to distribute to your beneficiaries (heirs) only that which remains in the trust estate after the passing of the surviving spouse.

> After the death of the Settlors, the balance of the principal shall be distributed in accordance with the provisions specified in the section of this Trust titled Allocation and Distribution.

[Decedent's Trust B]

If you are going to be using an A married or single form of trust, disregard this section completely.

The following clauses—Right to Income, Right to Principal, Discretionary Payments, Control of Assets, and Distribution of Residual of Trust B—set forth the rights afforded the surviving spouse under the decedent's Trust B section of an A-B or A-B-C revocable living trust.

[Decedent's Trust B shall be irrevocable and shall be held, administered, and distributed as follows:]

RIGHT TO INCOME

The decedent's Trust B holds the assets allocated to the deceased spouse. These assets "belong" to Trust B. Upon the passing of the first spouse, this trust becomes *irrevocable*. The surviving spouse cannot change the allocation or distribution to the beneficiaries of the deceased spouse. The surviving spouse does have certain rights associated with this division, one of which is the right to receive all the income generated by the assets in Trust B. This income must be used to maintain his or her standard of living and general well-being.

[Commencing with the date of deceased Spouse's death, the Trustee(s) shall pay to or apply for the benefit of the surviving Spouse during his or her lifetime all the net income from Trust B in convenient installments but no less frequently than quarterly.]

RIGHT TO PRINCIPAL

In addition to the above right of the surviving spouse to receive all of the income to Trust B, he or she has a right to access the principal as well.

If the income generated by the assets in Trust B is insufficient to maintain the "standard of living" and "well-being" of the surviving spouse, he or she has the right to spend the principal of this division. These funds are to be spent in maintaining the surviving spouse's "standard of living." The question you might be asking is, Who determines that standard of living? It is the surviving spouse. He/she can spend the entire Trust B estate providing for the same standard of living that the surviving spouse enjoyed when both husband and wife were living.

[The Trustee(s) may pay to, or apply for the benefit of, the surviving Spouse, during his or her lifetime, such sums from the principal of Trust B as in the Trustees' sole discretion shall be necessary or advisable from time to time for the medical care, education, and maintenance of the surviving Spouse, taking into consideration to the extent the Trustee deems advisable any other income or resources of the surviving Spouse known to the Trustee(s).]

133

DISCRETIONARY PAYMENTS

This is the third right to obtain income from the decedent's Trust B. It is referred to as the "frivolous right." The surviving spouse has a right to spend a predetermined amount in any fashion he or she wants. Unlike the other two rights above, there are no restrictions placed on how these funds may be spent.

[In addition to the income and discretionary payments of principal from this Trust, there shall be paid to the surviving Spouse, during his or her lifetime, from the principal of this Trust, upon the surviving Spouse's written request, during the last month of each fiscal year of the Trust an amount not to exceed during such fiscal year the amount of five thousand ($5,000) dollars or five (5%) percent of the aggregate value of principal for such fiscal year, whichever year, whichever is greater. This right of withdrawal is noncumulative, so that if the surviving Spouse does not withdraw, during such fiscal year, the full amount to which he or she is entitled under this Paragraph, his or her right to withdraw the amount not withdrawn shall lapse at the end of that fiscal year.]

CONTROL OF ASSETS

Even though the decedent's Trust B is irrevocable, the surviving spouse still has active management control over the nature of the assets in this trust.

[The surviving Spouse may, at any time by written notice, require the Trustee(s) either to make any nonproductive property of this Trust productive or to convert productive to nonproductive property, each within a reasonable time. The surviving Spouse may further require the Trustee(s) to invest part, or all, of this share of Trust assets for the purpose of maximizing income rather than growth, or growth rather than income.]

DISTRIBUTION OF RESIDUAL OF DECEDENT'S TRUST B

The surviving spouse cannot change the allocation and distribution to the beneficiaries of Trust B. This means that while he or she is the trustee of this trust, NO changes can be made that impact anyone who is an heir of this trust, what they are to receive, and when they are to receive their share or specific asset(s) from this trust.

Residual distribution means exactly that. The successor trustee(s) is/are going to distribute to your beneficiaries (heirs) only what remains in the trust estate after the passing of the surviving spouse.

[The balance of the principal of Trust B shall be distributed in accordance with the provisions specified in the section of this Trust titled Allocation and Distribution.

If the Spouse, whose share is represented by this Trust B, makes specific provision for beneficiaries, allocation, and distribution, and such provision cannot be complied with due to the death of a specified beneficiary, or if for any reason a specified distribution cannot be made as directed, then provisions of Per Stirpes, Intestate Succession, and Charity as specified herein shall govern distribution, with reference to the affected Settlor's beneficiaries and share.]

[Decedent's Trust C]

If you are going to be using an A married or A-B form of revocable living trust, disregard this section completely.

The following clauses—Right to Income, Right to Principal, Control of Assets, and Distribution of Residual of Trust C—set forth the rights afforded the surviving spouse under the decedent's Trust C section of an A-B-C married revocable living trust.

[Decedent's Trust C shall be irrevocable and shall be held, administered, and distributed as follows:]

RIGHT TO INCOME

The decedent's Trust C holds the assets allocated to the deceased spouse that are valued in excess of the deceased spouse's $600,000 personal estate exemption. These assets "belong" to Trust C. Upon the passing of the first spouse, this trust becomes *irrevocable*. The surviving spouse cannot change the allocation or distribution to the beneficiaries of the deceased spouse. The surviving spouse does have certain rights associated with Trust C, one of which is the right to receive all of the income generated by the assets in this trust. This income is to be used to maintain his or her standard of living and general well-being.

[Commencing with the date of Predeceased Spouse's death, the Trustee shall pay to or apply for the benefit of the surviving Spouse during his or her lifetime all the net income from Trust C in convenient installments but no less frequently than quarterly.]

RIGHT TO PRINCIPAL

In addition to the above right of the surviving spouse to receive all of the income to Trust C, he or she has a right to access the principal as well.

If the income generated by the assets in trusts B and C are insufficient to maintain the "standard of living" and "well-being" of the surviving spouse, he or she has the right to spend the principal of this division C. These funds are to be spent in maintaining the surviving spouse's "standard of living." Again, the surviving spouse determines that standard of living. He or she can spend the entire C Trust estate providing for the same standard of living and lifestyle that the surviving spouse enjoyed when both husband and wife were living.

[The Trustee may pay to, or apply for the benefit of, the surviving Spouse, during his or her lifetime, such sums from the principal of Trust C as in the Trustee's sole discretion shall be necessary or advisable from time to time for the medical care, education, and maintenance of the surviving Spouse, taking into consideration to the extent the Trustee deems advisable any other income or resources of the surviving Spouse known to the Trustee.]

CONTROL OF ASSETS

Again, even through the decedent's Trust C is irrevocable, the surviving spouse will still have active management control over the nature of the assets in this trust.

[The surviving Spouse may, at any time by written notice, require the Trustee either to make any nonproductive property of this trust productive or to convert productive property to nonproductive property, each within a reasonable time. The surviving Spouse may further require the Trustee to invest part, or all, of this share of Trust assets for the purpose of maximizing income rather than growth, or growth rather than income.]

DISTRIBUTION OF RESIDUAL OF TRUST C

The surviving spouse cannot change the allocation and distribution to the beneficiaries of Trust C. This means that while he or she is the Trustee of this trust, *no* changes can be made that affect the heirs of this trust, what they are to receive, and when they are to receive their share or specific assets(s) from this trust.

Residual distribution means exactly that. After the payment of inheritance, estate, or other taxes and expenses have been made, the successor trustee(s) is/are going to distribute to your beneficiaries (heirs) only that which remains in the trust estate after the passing of the surviving spouse.

[Upon the death of the surviving Settlor, the balance of Trust C shall be distributed as specified in Distribution of Residual of Trust C as constituted on the date of death of the first of the Settlors to die, giving effect to the original provisions of the Trust agreement and any amendments thereto then in existence.

If the Spouse whose share is represented by this Trust C makes specific provision for beneficiaries, allocation, and distribution, and such provision cannot be complied with due to the death of a specified beneficiary, or if for any reason a specified distribution cannot be made as directed, then provisions of Per Stirpes, Intestate Succession, and Charity as specified herein shall govern distribution, with reference to the affected Settlor's beneficiaries and share.]

Allocation and Distribution of Trust Assets

This following section on allocation and distribution acts much like a will in that in it you state:

1. Who the beneficiaries (heirs) of your trust estate are.
2. What they are to receive, either by share, value, or asset.
3. When they are to receive their inheritance to do with as they please.
4. Provisions for special circumstances, distributions, and asset management situations that may arise over the years as they relate to any heirs' beneficial interest in your trust estate.

The Trustees shall allocate, hold, administer, and distribute the Trust assets as hereinafter delineated.

UPON THE DEATH OF THE FIRST SETTLOR

Upon the passing of the first spouse, and if that spouse so directed, all or a portion of the trust estate assets can be distributed to that decedent's heirs.

Typically, though, all assets will remain held in the trust for the benefit of the surviving spouse. Such benefits to the surviving spouse have to be outlined earlier, and depend upon the type of trust used.

Upon the death of the first Settlor, YOUR NAME or SPOUSE'S NAME, the Trustee(s) shall make any separate distributions that have been specified by the deceased Settlor. The Trustee(s) shall also take into consideration the appropriate provisions of this section.

UPON THE DEATH OF BOTH SETTLORS

At the time both spouses have passed away, your trust becomes irrevocable. No changes can be made regarding any rights of named beneficiaries, unless provided for herein by the trustors.

At this point, the successor trustee or co-trustees will take over management control of the trust and its assets.

Upon the death of the surviving Spouse, the Trustee(s) shall hold, administer, and distribute the Trust in the following manner.

PERSONAL PROPERTY DISTRIBUTION

You can distribute small personal items, like your wedding ring or a family heirloom, by the below detailed procedure. This distribution technique is not to be used for major trust assets.

Memorandum
SPECIAL DISTRIBUTION OF PERSONAL PROPERTY

Description of Property   *Desired Recipient*

_____   _____

_____   _____

_____   _____

_____   _____

_____   _____

_____   _____

_____   _____

_____

Signature

_____   _____

_____   _____

_____   _____

_____   _____

_____   _____

_____   _____

_____   _____

_____

Signature

142

The Settlor requests the Trustee(s) to abide by any memorandum by the Settlor directing the disposition of personal and household effects of every kind including but not limited to furniture, appliances, furnishings, pictures, china, silverware, glass, books, jewelry, wearing apparel, and all policies of fire, burglary, property damage, and other insurance on or in connection with the use of this property. Otherwise, the personal and household effects of the Settlor(s) shall be distributed with the remaining assets of the trust estate.

RETENTION OF TRUST ASSETS

Customarily, all assets of the trust estate remain in trust until the youngest heir attains the age of twenty-one. This is done to keep the entire trust estate intact for the beneficial needs of all minor beneficiaries until they reach majority. In the event of an unusual occurrence, such as an extended illness, you might want the entire trust estate available to serve those specific needs of that child. When the youngest child attains age twenty-one, the trust estate will be available for allocation and distribution per the instructions set forth in your document. If you choose, you can change the specified age or delete this provision entirely.

When the youngest child of the Settlors, who is living, attains the age of twenty-one, the Trustee(s) shall divide the trust estate as then constituted into separate shares as hereinafter specified. This provision shall also apply to those shares allocated to the issue of a deceased primary beneficiary (as hereinafter designated).

SUPPORT AND EDUCATION

The trustee(s) is empowered to use trust estate assets to pay for continuation of a beneficiary's education until completed.

[At any time prior to the division of the Trust into shares as hereinbefore provided, or prior to distribution if divided, the Trustee(s) may, at its sole and absolute discretion, provide such sums as shall be necessary or advisable, for the care and maintenance, medical needs, and education of any primary beneficiary. This provision shall also apply to the issue of a deceased primary beneficiary (as hereinafter designated).]

EXTRAORDINARY DISTRIBUTION

With this clause, you grant the trustee(s) the power to provide funds, as they see fit, to pay for special objectives of any beneficiary of this trust. However, these payments will not diminish the allocated shares of any other beneficiary.

The Trustee(s) is/are further authorized, in their sole and absolute discretion, to provide such sums as shall be necessary or advisable, for the furtherance of worthwhile personal, professional, or business goals, and if deemed appropriate by the Trustee(s), to provide such reasonable sums for a partial or complete down payment on a home of any primary beneficiary, provided, however, that no such aid or support shall in any way diminish the benefits available to any other beneficiary. Such provision shall also apply to the issue of a deceased primary beneficiary of a Settlor.

GIFTS OR LOANS

You can make gifts and loans from the trust estate to any beneficiary. You should record which is a gift made outright and which is a loan to be repaid by the recipient. This repayment can be deducted from a beneficiary's allocated share.

The Trustee(s) shall reduce a beneficiary's share by any gifts or loans as shown in Schedule A.

SCHEDULE A

GIFTS AND LOANS

Gift or Loan?	Recipient	Amount	Date	Trustor's Initials
____	_____	_____	____	_____
____	_____	_____	____	_____
____	_____	_____	____	_____
____	_____	_____	____	_____
____	_____	_____	____	_____
____	_____	_____	____	_____
____	_____	_____	____	_____
____	_____	_____	____	_____
____	_____	_____	____	_____
____	_____	_____	____	_____
____	_____	_____	____	_____
____	_____	_____	____	_____
____	_____	_____	____	_____
____	_____	_____	____	_____

G - Gift
L - Loan

146

HANDICAPPED BENEFICIARIES

You are creating your trust for these main reasons:

1. To avoid government intrusion via the probate court.
2. To provide privacy for your family and affairs.
3. To obtain income tax benefits through the trust.
4. Where applicable, to minimize inheritance and estate tax liability.

In short, you want to keep it all (or as much as you possibly can) in the family. This next clause helps to further accomplish this estate planning goal.

What if one of your beneficiaries were to become handicapped and eligible for government benefits? You would not want to jeopardize that person's government benefits. Nor would you want to give Uncle Sam, or the state, the right to reach in and confiscate that beneficiary's share for repayment.

To prevent either of these occurrences from happening, you can remove that beneficiary from your trust and "disinherit" him or her. At the same time, the trustee is authorized, at his or her sole discretion, to provide whatever indirect funds are needed to provide personal care and maintenance for this handicapped individual.

In addition, you provide that should such handicapped individual recover, that person is automatically reinstated as your beneficiary.

Any beneficiary who is determined by a court of competent jurisdiction to be incompetent shall not have any discretionary rights of a beneficiary with respect to this Trust, or their share or portion thereof. The Trustee(s) shall hold and maintain such incompetent beneficiary's share of the trust estate and shall, in the Trustee's sole discretion, distribute for and provide for such beneficiary as provided for in this Trust for benefits to minors, and under Support and Education.

Notwithstanding the foregoing, any beneficiary who is diagnosed for the purposes of governmental benefits (as hereinafter delineated) as being not competent or as being disabled, and who shall be entitled to governmental support and benefits by any reason of such incompetency or disability, shall cease to be a beneficiary of this Trust. Likewise, they shall cease to be a beneficiary if any share or portion of the principal or income of the Trust shall become subject to the claims of any governmental agency for costs or benefits, fees or charges.

The portion of the trust estate which, absent the provisions of this section *Handicapped Beneficiaries*, would have been the share of such incompetent or handicapped person shall be retained in Trust for as long as that individual lives. The Trustee(s), at the sole discretion of the Trustee(s), may utilize such funds for the individual as specified under Support and Education. Upon the death of this individual, the residual of this share shall be distributed as otherwise specified in the Trust.

If such individual recovers from incompetency or disability, and is no longer eligible for aid from any governmental agency, including costs or benefits, fees or charges, such individual shall be reinstated as a beneficiary after sixty (60) days from such recovery, and the allocation and distribution provisions as stated herein shall apply to that portion of the trust estate which is held by the Trustee(s) subject to the foregoing provisions of this section.

If said handicapped beneficiary is no longer living and shall leave issue then living, the deceased handicapped beneficiary's share shall pass to said issue then living, equally. If there is no issue, such share shall be allocated proportionately among the remaining named beneficiaries.

Each share shall be distributed or retained in Trust as hereinafter provided.

PRIMARY BENEFICIARIES

You will need to identify those whom you wish to name as your primary beneficiaries. This is accomplished with this clause. Upon your passing, and that of your spouse, your primary beneficiaries will be allocated those shares, dollar value, and/or assets you have provided for.

If you want to exclude a certain individual or individuals, name them as being excluded as a beneficiary.

> Unless otherwise herein provided, upon or after the death of both of the Settlors, YOUR NAME and SPOUSE'S NAME, the primary beneficiary(ies) of this Trust are _____.

SPECIAL BEQUEST

A special bequest is a gift. It is generally an item of monetary value or specific dollar amount that may be distributed upon the passing of either husband or wife. Such bequest may come from separate property or from the joint estate. Special, or specific, bequests are distributed prior to the division of the estate into shares for the primary beneficiaries.

> The following special bequests shall be made by the Trustee(s) and distributed outright upon the death of the surviving Settlor: _____.

ALLOCATION OF TRUST ASSETS

Allocation deals with the way in which you, and your spouse, wish to have your estate divided among the beneficiaries at the passing of the surviving spouse. Allocations may be joint or separate, depending upon the beneficiaries of both spouses. Each of you can have the same or different beneficiaries.

In addition, each beneficiary may receive an equal share or an unequal share of the trust estate assets.

> Upon the death of the surviving Settlor, YOUR NAME or SPOUSE'S NAME, and after the debts and other obligations and provisions of the trust estate have been satisfied and any special distributions and retentions have been made, the Trustee(s) shall allocate the balance of the trust estate as then constituted (into————equal and separate shares as to provide one (1) share for each of the primary beneficiaries of this trust agreement).

Or if unequal allocation is desired, replace the above equal section with:

> (as follows: _____).
> If a primary beneficiary of the Settlors is not living, said share shall be allocated equally to the issue of such deceased primary beneficiary and distributed in accordance with the Provision titled Per Stirpes.

DISTRIBUTION OF TRUST ASSETS

In this section, you will be telling your successor trustee how the trust estate is to be distributed to your beneficiaries after the passing of the surviving spouse.

There are a number of ways these assets may be distributed. The form this distribution takes will determine how your beneficiaries will take possession. The most common means of distribution are:

1. Outright distribution upon the passing of the surviving spouse.
2. Distribution of income only with assets retained in trust to be distributed at a later date.
3. Deferred distribution at predetermined ages.
4. Distribution on a partial basis over a period of time.

The following includes examples of an outright and a deferred distribution.

OUTRIGHT DISTRIBUTION EXAMPLE

Upon the death of the surviving Settlor, the Trustee(s) shall distribute the trust estate allocated to the primary beneficiaries outright as soon as is practicable.

DEFERRED DISTRIBUTION EXAMPLE

Upon the death of the surviving Settlor, the Trustee(s) shall distribute the trust estate allocated to the primary beneficiaries as follows: When a primary beneficiary of the surviving Settlor attains the age of twenty-one (21) years, the Trustee(s) shall distribute to such named beneficiary one-third ($\frac{1}{3}$) of the principal of his or her share as then constituted. When said primary beneficiary attains the age of twenty-five (25) years, the Trustee(s) shall distribute to such named beneficiary one-half (½) of the principal of his or her share as then constituted. The Trustee(s) shall distribute to such named beneficiary the undistributed balance of his or her share when said primary beneficiary attains the age of twenty-nine (29) years.

If a named primary beneficiary has already attained age twenty-one (21), twenty-five (25), or twenty-nine (29) at the time this Trust is divided into shares, the Trustee(s) shall, upon making the division, distribute to such named beneficiary one-third (⅓), one-half (½), or all of his or her share, respectively.

Upon the death of a primary beneficiary, the Trustee(s) shall distribute the undistributed balance of the Estate as specified in other applicable provision herein included.

PER STIRPES

What happens in the event one of your designated primary beneficiaries is not living at the time of his or her distribution? If that primary beneficiary has children (issue), that portion of the trust estate allocated to the primary beneficiary will be distributed in equal shares to all living children of the deceased primary beneficiary.

The legal term for such form of distribution is per stirpes (pronounced: *per stir-peas*) and it applies to the issue of any designated beneficiary.

Typical distribution to such living issue will be split

153

into three parts. However, you can also distribute any share outright if you choose.

After division into shares pursuant to the paragraph Allocation of Trust Assets above, upon the death of a primary beneficiary of a Settlor prior to complete distribution of his or her share, the undistributed balance of such primary beneficiary's share shall be distributed per stirpes to his or her then living issue in the following manner: when such an heir (issue of a deceased primary beneficiary) attains the age of twenty-five (25) years, the Trustee(s) shall distribute to such beneficiary one-third (⅓) of the principal of his or her share as then constituted; and when an heir (issue of a deceased primary beneficiary) attains the age of thirty (30) years, the Trustee(s) shall distribute to such beneficiary one-half (½) of the principal of his or her share as then constituted; and when an heir (issue of a deceased primary beneficiary) attains the age of thirty-five (35) years, the Trustee(s) shall distribute to such beneficiary the undistributed balance of his or her share. If an heir (issue of a deceased primary beneficiary) has already attained age twenty-five (25), age thirty (30), or age thirty-five (35) at the time this Trust is divided into shares, the Trustee shall, upon making the division, distribute to such beneficiary one-third (⅓), two-thirds (⅔), or all of his or her share, respectively. If a deceased primary beneficiary should leave no issue, then said deceased primary beneficiary's share shall be distributed per stirpes to a Settlor's then living issue.

INTESTATE SUCCESSION

The laws of intestate succession apply only when all named beneficiaries and their issue are deceased at the time of the distribution of your estate. Upon such occurrence, your estate would be distributed to living family members such as your brothers, sisters, nieces, nephews, etc. You can name other individuals instead of family members.

If at the time of a Settlor's death, or at any later time prior to final distribution hereunder, all of a Settlor's beneficiaries are deceased and no other disposition of the property is directed by this Trust, then and in that event the then remaining property of this Trust shall be distributed to a Settlor's heirs by right of intestate succession (except that no amounts shall be allocated or distributed to the parents of a Settlor).

CHARITY

You may elect to circumvent the above clause by naming specific charities you select to receive the balance of your trust estate. Each spouse may choose different charities.

If no such heirs are extant, then the Trustee(s) is directed to distribute the property to qualified nonprofit charitable organizations identified in Schedule B. If no such charity is identified in Schedule B, the Trustee(s) shall select appropriate nonprofit charitable organizations for distribution of the trust estate.

General Provisions

The following section incorporates general provisions that you will probably want in your trust document. They are general in nature and may apply to all situations.

The following general provisions apply to the entire trust agreement.

INTENTION TO AVOID PROBATE

Should the situation change dramatically, your successor trustee and executor can elect to probate your estate if they believe that action would benefit the estate and its heirs.

It is the intention of the Trustors, YOUR NAME and SPOUSE'S NAME, to avoid probate through the use of this trust agreement. If, however, the Trustee(s) of this Trust and the Executor(s) of the estate of either or both Trustors shall mutually determine that it shall be in the best interest of the beneficiaries of the Trust, and the beneficial interests of the beneficiaries shall not thereby be altered, the Trustee(s) may subject any asset to probate to accomplish a result unavailable without probate (e.g., to bar future creditor claims).

ANNUAL ACCOUNTING

If the assets of the trust estate are not distributed outright, the beneficiaries have a right to receive an annual accounting as to the status of the assets being held in trust for them. This can be as simple as providing a bank statement.

The Successor Trustee(s) shall render an annual accounting to the beneficiary or beneficiaries of the Trust not more than one hundred twenty (120) days following the close of the fiscal year of the Trust.

PARTIAL INVALIDITY

This clause is self-explanatory.

> If any provision of this trust agreement is void, invalid, or unenforceable, the remaining provisions shall nevertheless be valid and carried into effect.

HEADINGS

This clause is self-explanatory.

> The headings of this agreement are for convenience only and are not a part of the text.

COUNTERPARTS

This clause is self-explanatory.

> This trust agreement may be executed in any number of counterparts and each shall constitute an original of one and the same instrument.

SPENDTHRIFT PROVISIONS

A beneficiary of this trust cannot pledge, nor can a creditor of that beneficiary attach, his or her future inheritance.

Except as otherwise provided herein, all payments of principal and income payable, or to become payable, to the beneficiary of any Trust created hereunder shall not be subject to anticipation, assignment, pledge, sale, or transfer in any manner, nor shall any said beneficiary have the power to anticipate or encumber such interest, nor shall such interest, while in the possession of the Trustee(s), be liable for, or subject to, the debts, contracts, obligations, liabilities, or torts of any beneficiary.

SIMULTANEOUS DEATH

If you, your spouse, and/or a beneficiary should pass away at the same time, the state will assume an order of passing that maximizes the tax liability of the estate. This clause stops them.

If both Settlors, YOUR NAME and SPOUSE'S NAME, should die under circumstances which would render it doubtful as to which Settlor died first, it shall be conclusively presumed for the purposes of this Trust that the wife died first. If any other beneficiary and a Settlor should die under such circumstances, it shall be conclusively presumed that said beneficiary predeceased such Settlor by sixty (60) days.

LAST ILLNESS AND FUNERAL EXPENSE

This clause is self-explanatory.

> On the death of any person entitled to income or support from any Trust hereunder, the Trustee(s) shall be authorized to pay the funeral expenses and the expenses of the last illness of such person from the corpus of the trust estate from which such person was entitled to income or support.

Glossary of Terms

This section defines certain terms that will circumvent legal arguments as to definitions.

> The Glossary of Terms covers three basic categories: Trustee, Child or Children, and Internal Revenue Code Terminology.

TRUSTEE

This clause is self-explanatory.

> Whenever the word "Trustee" or any modifying or substituted pronoun therefore is used in this Trust, such words and respective pronouns shall be held and taken to include both the singular and the plural, the masculine, feminine, and neuter gender thereof, and shall apply equally to the Trustee named herein and to any successor or substitute Trustee acting hereunder, and such successor or substitute Trustee shall possess all the rights, powers and duties, authority and responsibility conferred upon the Trustee originally named herein.

CHILD OR CHILDREN

If you have no issue (children), disregard the section.

> For the purpose of this trust, "children" means the lawful blood descendants in the first degree of either or both Settlors, YOUR NAME and SPOUSE'S NAME; and "issue" and "descendants" mean the lawful blood descendants in any degree of the ancestor designated; provided, however, that if a person has been adopted, that person shall be considered a child of such adopting parent and such adopted child and his or her issue shall be considered as issue of the adopting

parent or parents and of anyone who is by blood or adoption an ancestor of the adopting parent or either of the adopting parents. The terms "child," "children," "issue," "descendant" and "descendants," or those terms preceded by the terms "living" or "then living," shall include the lawful blood descendant in the first degree of either or both Settlors even though such descendant is born after the death of a Settlor.

INTERNAL REVENUE CODE TERMINOLOGY

This clause is self-explanatory.

As used herein, the words "gross estate," "adjusted gross estate," "taxable estate," "unified credit," "state death tax credit," "maximum marital deduction," "marital deduction," "qualified terminable interest," "qualified terminable interest property," and any other word or words which from the context in which it or they are used refer to the Internal Revenue Code shall be assigned the same meaning as such words have for the purpose of applying the Internal Revenue Code to a deceased Settlor's estate. Reference to sections of the Internal Revenue Code shall refer to the Internal Revenue Code amended to the date of such Settlor's death.

Creation and Termination of Trust

In this section, you set forth those items that further define the trust and its functioning.

This trust agreement is created in its state of execution, however, it is intended to be effective in all states and foreign jurisdictions where it owns property of any kind or value.

SITUS OF TRUST

Your trust can be transferred from one state to another with no loss of benefit or power.

The situs of the trust estate may be transferred from YOUR STATE OF RESIDENCE to such other jurisdiction within the United States as the majority of the income beneficiaries may designate only with the approval of the Trustee(s). While the situs of the Trust is in YOUR STATE OF RESIDENCE, YOUR STATE OF RESIDENCE law will govern the Trust provisions.

TERMINATION OF TRUST

There are laws against trusts existing in perpetuity. Consequently, as your trust cannot last forever, it must cease to exist at some point. In this clause, you set up the time frame and mechanism to terminate the trust.

> Notwithstanding anything herein to the contrary, the Trust created hereunder shall terminate not later than twenty-one (21) years after the death of the last survivor of the surviving Settlor and any other beneficiary or beneficiaries named or defined in this Trust living on the date of the predeceased Spouse's death, when the Trustee(s) shall distribute each remaining Trust hereunder to the beneficiary or beneficiaries of the current income thereof; and if there is more than one beneficiary, in the proportion in which they are beneficiaries; or if no proportion is designated, in equal shares to such beneficiaries.

AGREEMENT BETWEEN PARTIES

You (and your spouse) are, in effect, setting up a contract when you create your revocable living trust. It is this contractual relationship that provides the significant trustee powers needed to control the trust estate. As such (both of) you need to affirm your intentions to enter into this agreement.

This is to witness that I, YOUR NAME, and I, SPOUSE'S NAME, have read the provisions of this trust agreement and understand the provisions therein, and it is our intent to enter into this trust agreement in accordance with any and all YOUR STATE OF RESIDENCE civil code sections, allowing a husband and wife to enter into a contract with each other regarding community property or quasi-community property.

IN WITNESS WHEREOF, the provisions of this Declaration of Trust shall bind YOUR NAME and SPOUSE'S NAME as Trustors, and YOUR NAME or SPOUSE'S NAME as Trustees; Successor Trustee(s) assuming the role of Trustee hereunder, and the beneficiaries of this Trust as well as their successors and assigns.

Dated at YOUR TOWN OF RESIDENCE, YOUR STATE OF RESIDENCE, (DATE OF SIGNING).

TRUSTORS: TRUSTEES:

_____   _____

(Sign and print your   (Sign and print your
name)   name)

_____   _____
(Sign and print   (Sign and print
Spouse's name)   Spouse's name)

**THE SIGNING OF YOUR TRUST
DOCUMENT MUST BE NOTARIZED OR
OFFICIALLY ACKNOWLEDGED, NOT
MERELY WITNESSED.**

COMPETENCY CLAUSE

The following is an important addendum to your trust. In it, you may choose the medical personnel you want to determine your competency should it be called into question someday. Their evaluation can always be challenged.

By providing this choice, you can bypass a court proceeding to determine your competency. This allows the family to maintain control during an emotional and stressful time.

In addition, you can make changes as time goes on by simply striking out a current name and replacing it with a new name.

Each spouse should complete a competency clause and attach it to the trust document.

Competency Clause Addendum
Appointment of Physicians to Determine Competency

The undersigned Trustor hereby appoints the following as physicians to determine the Trustor's competency to serve as Trustee under this Trust.

(NAME OF FIRST DOCTOR) (ADDRESS OF FIRST DOCTOR) (CITY, STATE, AND ZIP)	(NAME OF SECOND DOCTOR) (ADDRESS OF SECOND DOCTOR) (CITY, STATE, AND ZIP)

The above appointed physicians shall serve until this appointment shall be amended or revoked by separate writing of the affected Trustor.

Dated: _____

_____
YOUR NAME OR SPOUSE'S NAME

The undersigned Trustor hereby appoints the following physicians to determine the Trustor's competency to serve as Trustee under this Trust.

_____	_____
Name	Name
_____	_____
Address	Address
_____	_____
City/State	City/State

The above appointed physicians shall serve until this appointment shall be amended or revoked by separate writing of the affected Trustor.

_____	_____
Date	Date
_____	_____
Signed	Signed

Please Note: If fewer than two physicians are named above, or if either or both of the named physicians are unable or unwilling to serve, the "Attorney in Fact" appointed under a Durable Power of Attorney is authorized to name such Physician(s).

Other Control Issues

For the majority of Americans, the revocable living trust is the foundation of proper estate planning. It is the vital tool that makes it possible to avoid probate, unnecessary taxes and legal fees, and helps protect your loved ones from undue emotional distress.

Additionally, there are other documents of vital importance that you might want to consider if you plan to provide a full measure of protection for your family.

These documents are designed to protect your family in the event of a medical emergency or for some other reason that might render you incapable of handling your own affairs. They will complement your trust and are compatible with your trust.

These documents include the following:

DURABLE POWER OF ATTORNEY FOR ASSET MANAGEMENT

In this document, you designate an individual to manage your affairs in the event you're unable to do so. For example, if you have any assets outside of your trust, the person named in your durable power of attorney for asset management will have the power to transfer those particular assets into your trust. Upon regaining your ability to make decisions for yourself, your control over your nontrust assets is reinstated.

DURABLE POWER OF ATTORNEY FOR HEALTH CARE

This document is another important adjunct to your overall estate planning. With it, you may appoint an individual to make medical and health care decisions on your behalf in the event you are unable to make them for yourself.

For instance, let's say that you were in an automobile accident and injured severely enough to have lapsed into a coma; that person named in your durable power of attorney for health care would have the power to give consent for any and all medical procedures the doctors determined could be performed in your best interest. The ability of a family member or close friend to make these types of decision could literally save your life. Once you regain your capacity to make decisions yourself, this power is revested with you.

I sincerely hope that you will never need to use the protection afforded by the durable power of attorney, nomination of conservator, or living will. However, experience has shown that if you should ever need these important documents in an emergency, and didn't have them already prepared prior to your unforeseen need, it is just too late to prepare them. You and your family will lose important control, and an already stressful situation will be made needlessly worse.

LAST WILL AND TESTAMENT (POUR OVER WILL)

Another document you might consider having drawn is your last will and testament. You might be a little confused about now because I have been saying all along that you really don't want a "will." Let me explain: the pour over will is a will with a very big difference from a typical will. Think of a pour over will as your estate's safety net. Should you forget to transfer an asset into your trust, this pour over will catches that asset and "pours it over" into your trust. It ensures that nothing slips through the cracks. This is accomplished by naming your trust as the beneficiary of your pour over will. Once that asset is in your trust, it will be allocated and distributed to your heirs as stipulated in your trust.

One word of caution about using a pour over will. As stated, it is to be used only as a safety net, and not as an excuse to leave assets outside your trust.

If the dollar value or type of assets outside of your trust exceeds the minimum probate amount, or exempt category, in your state of residence, and where you may hold property, those assets will have to be probated *before* pouring over into your living trust. The power of the living trust is based on your putting assets into it before your passing.

ASSIGNMENT OF PERSONAL PROPERTY AND BILL OF SALE

To be effective, your living trust should "own" *all* of your assets, excluding a small day-to-day checking account and, in some states, your automobile. These assets include your personal property, from your furniture to the clothes on your back. If you assign them into your trust, they will never be in jeopardy of triggering a probate of your estate. A properly drawn assignment of personal property and bill of sale should be a "blanket assignment" with no inventory required.

This type of instrument covers all of the personal property you currently own and any you will ever own. Again, no inventory is required when you use this type of assignment, and your control of those assets will not diminish.

Estate Organization: Summing It Up

A very important part of proper estate planning is asset and document organization. You need to have a very simple, yet effective, way of organizing your important documents and assets. It should provide you and your successors with a "one-stop" system to find any and all needed documentation and information.

The best tool to accomplish this is to have an "estate organizer." I have found that the most effective organizer is a three-ring loose-leaf binder. This binder should include section dividers, and have pockets on both inside front and back covers.

This powerful organizing tool should contain the following documents and information:

1. Copies of all correspondence concerning the transferring of trust assets.
2. Any important business cards associated with your estate planning.
3. One signed *original* of your living trust docu-

ment. It is important that any documents be "backed up" with a duplicate set, with original signatures, stored at a different location than your home. If one set is destroyed in a fire, you will have a second duplicate set of these important documents.

Make sure that your successor trustee knows that you have set up a living trust and the location of the duplicate set of your living trust documents. If you were to perish in the fire that destroyed your home set of documents, your heirs would be hard-pressed to settle your estate without probate. Ask your estate planner if he or she provides a document archive service for their living trust clients.

4. An abstract of your trust. This is a document that provides banks and financial institutions all the information they should need to set up trust accounts.

    In addition, it keeps prying eyes from seeing those parts of your trust that are none of their concern.

5. Assignment of personal property and bill of sale.

6. Memorandum of personal property. This device is used to give small personal items, such as a family heirloom, to a named individual. It does not cover major trust assets.

7. Last will and testament (pour over will).

8. A final instructions page. This is a checklist for funeral arrangements, special notifications, special instructions from you, and a settlement "to-do" list for your surviving or successor trustee(s).

9. A directory of the phone and mailing address of

any and all people you would want and need notified of your passing.

10. A personal data profile that records your personal information, such as your birth date and place, Social Security number, and the names of your parents and children.

11. Durable power of attorney for asset management.

12. Durable power of attorney for health care.

13. Nomination of conservator.

14. Living will, right-to-die clause.

15. Guardianship for your children. This includes adult handicapped children.

16. A brief financial statement of your estate's estimated value. This should be updated once every year or two.

17. A savings and investment section containing voided photocopies of the following:

> Checking accounts
> Saving accounts
> Credit union accounts
> Money market accounts
> Certificates of deposit
> Treasury bills
> Stock and bond certificates
> Mutual funds
> Notes receivable
> Tax-deferred retirement plans
> Profit-sharing plans
> Individual retirement accounts
> Keogh plans
> Tax-sheltered annuities

18. Copies of all real estate deeds, recorded and un-recorded, and a property tax bill for each parcel.
19. The face page of all insurance policies.
20. Gift/loan accounting section.
21. Business agreements and documentation.

Estate Settlement

With a properly drawn revocable living trust and your estate organized in the above manner, your surviving spouse or heirs should know how to settle your estate in about one hour. It's true.

Everything they need to settle your estate will be right there at their fingertips, all information and the power to act. Really, it can be that simple. I have seen it happen time and time again.

What more loving gift could you give your spouse and family than the ability to avoid probate and maintain complete control.

The loss of a loved one is a shattering experience. There is no way to soften the pain. Why make it more painful by subjecting your spouse and family to probate, when probate is unnecessary? Having a living trust will shield your family from the additional pain and agony of probate.

The living trust is truly a gift of love.

Reviewing the Perils
of Probate One More Time,
or
What You Don't Know Can
Hurt You

You've probably done a fine job of building your estate. You may own your home, have money invested in marketable securities, and a savings account. Perhaps you own bank accounts, stocks, etc. Besides, there are the other problems of joint tenancy that we examined earlier.

Caution! Joint tenant ownership does not avoid probate, it merely *defers* probate until the passing of the surviving joint tenant.

Joint Tenant Tax Trap

There are also some very negative aspects of joint tenant ownership that relate to the paying of unnecessary income taxes on the sale of capital assets. "Capital assets" include real estate, stocks, coins, etc. For the purposes of this illustration, let's use a private home purchased a number of years ago for $50,000. That

$50,000 becomes your *cost basis* of the property. Assume that in today's real estate market, the home has a *market value* of $200,000 (market value being the price you could expect to receive for your property).

The difference between the cost basis and the market value is called a *capital gain,* which, in our example, amounts to $150,000 in appreciation on that home. To put it bluntly, the government considers you made a "profit" on that home, so it's subject to capital gains tax.

Market value = $200,000
Cost basis = 50,000
Capital Gains = $150,000

How joint tenant ownership affects that capital gain can be very taxing. If you are a married couple and hold title to your home as joint tenants, the IRS has a surprise for you when the first spouse passes away.

For income tax purposes, Uncle Sam divides your home right down the center. They can do this because joint tenant ownership is nothing more than "equal ownership" under the law. You do not own a "whole" home valued at $200,000, you own only one-half and your spouse owns the second half. The original cost basis gets halved, so your half is $25,000 and your spouse's half is $25,000.

COST BASIS
$50,000

$25,000 $25,000
You   Your Spouse

177

MARKET VALUE
$200,000

"Profits" $75,000 $75,000
             You   Your Spouse

When the first spouse dies, the serious tax implications of holding title as joint tenants become evident. Upon the death of the first, one-half the property will receive a special tax break called "stepped-up valuation." This means that his/her original cost basis will be "stepped up" to the market value of his/her half as of the date of that spouse's passing.

Original, or "old" cost basis   = $ 25,000
Stepped-up or "new" cost basis = $100,000

This tax break is not given to the surviving spouse. He/she does not qualify because this tax break is given at death only and the surviving spouse is still alive.

As the surviving joint tenant, the spouse receives your half of the home outside of probate by right of survivor. Together with the half he/she owns, the spouse is now sole owner of a home valued at $200,000.

In addition, the spouse would also "inherit" the deceased spouse's new stepped-up cost basis. Combining the "new" cost basis and the spouse's "old" cost basis, the "adjusted" cost basis is $125,000.

"New" cost basis   = $100,000
Surviving spouse's "old" cost basis = +$25,000
Adjusted cost basis   = $125,000

Assume the house is now too large, filled with too many memories, so the surviving spouse sells it for $200,000. The IRS will deduct the cost basis from the sales price. The result will show a capital gain of $75,000.

Sales price   = $200,000
Adjusted cost basis = − $125,000
Capital gains   = $75,000

However, the $75,000 "profit" may be taxed as ordinary income in the year it was received. Looking at a 1994 federal income tax rate of 39 percent, and applicable state income tax, which, for example, is 15 percent in New York, it could amount to a 54 percent tax bite.

Dollars Lost Because of Poor Estate Planning

Take the same home, but this time you own it as community, or common, property, or sole ownership property. Under community property ownership and sole property ownership, the IRS can no longer come in and divide your home in half. This is because community property is "common" ownership and sole property is singular ownership. Your ownership of the home is one unit and cannot be divided. If married, each spouse owns 100 percent of the home, all $200,000 worth. They also share the original cost basis of $50,000.

Upon the passing of the first spouse (if married), the original cost basis of $50,000 gets "stepped up" to the full $200,000. If the surviving spouse sells the home, the tax liability will be strikingly different. The same holds true for sole ownership of property.

Sales price   = $200,000
Stepped-up or "new" cost basis = − $200,000
Taxable capital gain   =   -0-

Since there is no "capital gain," there are no income or capital gain taxes due. By holding title to your home in community property, common property, or sole property, you eliminated all income tax liability upon the sale of that asset. *Your spouse is almost $31,000 richer.*

By holding title to your home and property in a living trust at the time of your passing away, your spouse will have the benefits of both worlds—not only avoiding probate, but also owing no income taxes on the sale of capital assets.

If your surviving spouse chooses not to sell the property, and subsequently passes away, your family will avoid probate a second time and obtain a second full stepped-up cost basis with all the tax benefits on the sale of capital assets.

Creating Your Living Trust

Obviously, the most effective way to avoid probate and the joint tenant tax situation is to create a living trust. The most widely used trust is the revocable living trust, which is also referred to as the family trust and inter vivos trust.

A trust is a legal "entity." It is a paper person. As such, it can do nothing for itself. It needs someone to act on its behalf, to manage and administer the trust estate and take care of trust business. These parties that act on behalf of the trust are called trustees. Typically, you will be the trustee of your own living trust. If you are married, the husband and the wife are, in most cases, joint trustees.

After you have set up your living trust, your next step is to "fund" your trust. Funding a trust involves putting assets into the trust so that your trust owns those assets. This is easily accomplished by switching ownership of these assets into the name of your living trust. This is critically important. To avoid probate, the assets must be *owned* by your living trust.

Reminder! While you are alive and are the trustees of your own revocable living trust, you remain in total control of your assets. No special accounting needed.

After both spouses (who are also trustees) pass away, the trust becomes an *irrevocable living trust*. The successor trustees are now legally bound by a "fiduciary" responsibility to make certain your wishes are carried out as to the trust directions.

After division and distribution of all the trust assets,

the trust will be void of assets with jurisdiction over nothing. Hence, it will cease to exist as a funded entity.

While your living trust was in effect, it accomplished eight major goals:

1. It helped you structure the title to your assets for your beneficial use while still under your control.
2. For married couples, it protected the estate from probate upon the passing of the first spouse.
3. It provided for the spouse to remain in control of the trust's affairs.
4. In a married trust, upon the passing of the second spouse, it shielded the family from probate a second time.
5. It provided full family control of the trust estate.
6. It accomplished the orderly transition from the surviving spouse to the successor trustee(s).
7. Allocation and distribution plans for your beneficiaries were carried out per your instructions.
8. Where applicable, it gave surviving spouse and family significant tax benefits (capital gains), plus estate and/or inheritance tax benefits.

These points are the essence of proper planning.

Questions and Answers Regarding Living Trusts

1. *Do I need to file a separate income tax return for my living trust?*

   NO. As long as the entire trust remains revocable (while the original trustors are living), no separate tax filing is required. You will simply report all income from the trust on your personal income tax return. A revocable living trust is called a grantor trust by the IRS. As such, all income to the trust is considered income to you, and is accounted for and taxed accordingly.

   Only *after* the passing of an original trustor is a separate, simple federal trust tax return (Form 1041) required and filed.

2. *Will I need to register my living trust?*

   NO. One of the benefits of your living trust is the total privacy it provides. No governmental agency or court needs to know you have a living trust.

3. *Can my living trust be amended if my situation changes? If so, is it easy?*

   YES. If you need to make a major change in your living trust, this is easily accomplished with a written amendment. Make sure to have your signature notarized to prevent fraud. It is advisable that you review your living trust every couple of years to ensure that it still reflects your needs and goals.

4. *Can my living trust shelter my regular income from income taxes?*

    NO. A revocable living trust is not a device to shelter your income from income taxes. This is because you remain in control of your assets, and any income from those assets, as well as all applicable income, will be taxed to you personally. *However*, your living trust can provide full "stepped-up basis" on the sale of certain assets, thereby avoiding income taxes. In addition, it provides protection, where applicable, from estate taxes upon your passing.

5. *If I transfer my home into my living trust, will it be reassessed, requiring me to pay higher property taxes?*

    NO. Transferring your home into your living trust is usually exempt from reassessment. Check with your local property tax authorities.

6. *Will I lose any income tax deductions by transferring assets into my living trust?*

    NO. All such deductions remain personal to you and will be accounted for just as they are now. No special accounting is needed.

7. *Is the cost of my living trust tax deductible?*

    YES. Currently, 80 percent of the cost of preparing your living trust and asset transfers are an estate planning expense deduction, subject to limitations on Schedule A on your federal return. State exemptions may also apply.

8. *Is there a cost in transferring assets into my living trust?*

YES and NO. Except for the preparing and recording of your new trust transfer deeds and business assignments, there should be no costs involved. If you retain an estate planning professional to prepare your living trust, that person will usually prepare (and record) the new deeds and assignments for a small additional fee. Banks, financial institutions, and stock brokerages should not charge you to reregister accounts in the name of your living trust.

9. *Do I need to have my assets appraised before transferring them into my living trust?*

NO. Although it is wise to have a good estimate of the value of your assets, formal and costly appraisals are not necessary.

10. *Can I sell assets once they are placed in my living trust?*

YES. Absolutely. As long as you are the controlling trustee(s), you have complete authority over the purchase and sale of those assets.

11. *Can I revoke (terminate) my living trust?*

YES. This is a revocable living trust. Should it become necessary (for example, due to a divorce), you may revoke your living trust simply and completely.

12. *Should I transfer my personal property (furniture, clothes, jewelry, etc.) into my living trust?*

   THAT DEPENDS. Although not absolutely necessary, it is recommended. Outside your living trust, if your personal property exceeds the probate minimum in your state, those assets could be forced to go through probate. Assigning them to your living trust avoids this possibility. It would be wise to check with the clerk of the probate court in your county to find out what this minimum probate limit is.

13. *Do I transfer my IRA, Keoghs, retirement accounts, and life insurance policies into my living trust?*

   NO. These assets will not be subject to probate if you have named a beneficiary, other than assigning them to your estate. Depending on circumstances, you may wish to name your living trust as the contingent beneficiary of these assets.

14. *Do I need to place my safe deposit box in my living trust?*

   NO. This is not necessary. However, to be on the safe side, it wouldn't hurt to do so. This will help to prevent confusion later on.

15. *Is there anything I do not transfer to my living trust?*

   YES. You do not need to transfer a moderately valued automobile into the trust. The Department of Motor Vehicles in your state probably allows heirs to transfer an automobile upon your passing. Check with local authorities. Also, you can maintain a personal checking account in your own name, as long as its value, along with all other assets held outside of your living trust, does not exceed the minimum probate limit.

16. *Will a revocable living trust protect me from my creditors?*

   NO. Since you have total control over the trust estate while you are alive, your creditors can still reach these assets. However, if you have a living trust structured for a married couple, after the first spouse passes away, part of your living trust becomes irrevocable, making it possible to shield those assets from your creditors.

17. *Is it easy to "settle" an estate after one or both spouses pass away?*

   YES. If your living trust is properly drawn, fully funded, and your estate organized, very little effort will be required to execute the transfers necessary to carry out the provisions of the trust and settle your estate. The process can be accomplished by the family without any outside help. In many cases, an estate can be "settled" in less than one hour. If desired, your estate planning professional can help the family settle your estate.

18. *Can I prevent my assets from going to my children's spouses?*

YES. Assets you give your children are their sole and separate property. Once you have given those assets outright to your children, you have no control over them. If your children choose to commingle these assets, all or part of these assets could very well end up leaving your bloodline. If you want to minimize this, consider retaining these assets in trust to be distributed periodically.

19. *Are there disadvantages to a living trust?*

YES, THREE.

1. There are "up front" costs of preparing and funding your living trust. By comparison, a simple will is less expensive to prepare. On the "back end," after a death, probate of a will takes a healthy bite out of assets in an estate, while there is almost no cost to transferring assets in a living trust.

2. There is a more "up front" paperwork in setting up and funding a living trust. But once this is completed, it's over. Consider a living trust a form of insurance to protect your estate from the cost of probate, taxes, and loss of family control.

3. Under the new federal budget, income to trust funds, held for deferred distribution, will now be taxed at a higher rate. The old rate started at 31 percent on income above $11,250; the new rate increased to 39.6 percent on income of $7,500 or more. These new changes in the tax rate, as they apply to trust funds, might subject those funds to a higher tax liability than if they were held by the beneficiary. If you think these new rates apply to you, seek advice from your own tax adviser.

20. *If I decide to set up a trust, how do I choose which type to use? What should it cost me?*

There are many kinds and sizes of hammers. When you buy a particular hammer, its price is not based on the number of nails it will drive over the ensuing years, the price of a hammer is fixed. Similarly, like the hammer, you buy the trust that will do the job for you.

If you are a single individual, the only revocable living trust the IRS allows you to use is an A-type single living trust.

The use of an A married, A-B married, or A-B-C married (QTIP) Living Trust depends on the anticipated value of the estate upon the passing of the first spouse. These documents are "tools" designed to fulfill a task based on a set of factors. As such, the value of an estate *within the protection ranges* afforded by each document type (A, A-B, A-B-C) should not drive the price. Depending on the scope of the living trust package, the following pricing should apply nationwide if prepared by professional estate planners. Please remember that some estate planners are attorneys who may charge an attorney's hourly rates, possibly from $150 to $300 per hour, or more. You might want to find a professional who will prepare your trust on a flat-fee basis acceptable to you rather than an hourly rate. The following rates are to be used as a guideline only.

An A single living trust package should cost between $445 and $795.

An A married living trust package should cost between $575 and $945.

An A-B married living trust package will range from $745 to $1,095.

An A-B-C (QTIP) married living trust package should be between $975 and $1,345.

There should be no other costs associated with setting up and funding the living trust *except* for those people who are transferring real estate and business interests into it.

21. *Do state and local governments tax estates?*

YES, SOME DO. Depending on the "situs" state of the living trust, there may be additional estate or death taxes levied by that state. In states classified as "federal credit," "federal exempt," or "pick up," there are no additional estate taxes over and above those paid to the federal government upon the passing of an individual.

Twenty-seven states come under this *tax exempt* status: Alabama, Alaska, Arizona, Arkansas, California, Colorado, Florida, Georgia, Hawaii, Idaho, Illinois, Maine, Minnesota, Missouri, Montana, Nevada, New Hampshire, New Mexico, North Dakota, Oregon, Texas, Utah, Vermont, Virginia, Washington, West Virginia, and Wyoming.

The other twenty-three states levy an estate tax upon a death. This is in addition to any federal inheritance tax that might be due. The *tax collecting* states are: Connecticut, Delaware, Indiana, Iowa, Kansas, Kentucky, Louisiana, Maryland, Massachusetts, Michigan, Mississippi, Nebraska, New Jersey, New York, North Carolina, Ohio, Oklahoma, Pennsylvania, Rhode Island, South Carolina, South Dakota, Tennessee, and Wisconsin.

The estate tax levy is different in every state imposing this form of tax. The laws, codes, and regulations governing such taxation change frequently. Contact a local source in your state of residence and other states where you own property to obtain specific threshold, rate, and exemption information that applies to your particular situation. An accountant should be a good source for this information.

22. *Can I still make gifts and set up trust funds for my children and grandchildren?*

YES. With or without a living trust, one's ability to make a $10,000 annual, tax-free gift to one person is the same. Currently, the number of annual gifts one can make is not set by law. There is an ongoing discussion of limiting the number of tax-free gifts an individual can make to three.

There are different ways of setting up a trust fund account for grandchildren or other family members. The simplest, most common method is to use the power inherent in the living trust. A properly drawn revocable living trust is an excellent vehicle for establishing ongoing management of a trust fund.

Under a will, an heir receives all of his/her inheritance outright upon settlement of the probate. If the heir is a minor or incompetent, the probate court will require that a controlled trust be established for the benefit of said heir until such time as the heir attains the age of majority or is determined by the court to be competent.

On the other hand, after the passing of a trustor(s), a living trust can hold assets for the benefit of an heir for years while providing for periodic distributions.

Another way to transfer assets to grandchildren is to set up a generation-skipping trust as outlined previously in this book. Their effectiveness as it relates to tax savings has been considerably diminished by the Budget Reconciliation Act of 1993. Tax free is not really tax free. In a generation-skipping trust, the transferor pays one generation's worth of federal inheritance tax at the maximum rate of 50 percent. Caution is advised, as there can even be a double tax situation created under certain conditions.

One can also establish trusts for minors under IRS Code Sections 2503(b) and (c). They provide only for minors, and as such are limited in their usefulness.

23. *Is money received through an inheritance taxable?*

NO. Inheritance always passes to the heir federal income tax free.

24. *Shouldn't everyone have a will?*

YES. Anyone who has an estate and/or owns property should have a will at the very least. It is better than not having provided for any estate planning at all. But having a will is only a half-step in the right direction. A will establishes a degree of distribution control in estate planning. Unfortunately, people believe that a will protects them from probate. It does not.

A properly drawn living trust, in essence, becomes a "will." In it, the trustor(s) provides for both allocation and distribution of the estate. The pour over will, which should accompany your trust, names your living trust as the beneficiary of any assets inadvertently left "outside" of that trust. Upon the passing of the trustor(s), those particular assets will "pour over" into the trust, and be distributed as set forth in the living trust document. Caution is the watchword when one uses this type of will. The value of the assets to be "poured over" may trigger probate of the pour over will. It should be considered as a safety net only, and not as an excuse for not funding the trust.

25. *Can I avoid probate entirely?*

YES. Briefly, there are three ways to avoid probate. First is to own nothing in your name or have an estate valued at below the probate threshold of your state where you hold title to an asset. The concept of "owning nothing" is, in essence, the benefit of a living trust.

The second avoidance method shields an estate from probate. You, *as an individual*, own nothing. Your living trust, a legal entity or "paper person," owns it all. Upon your passing, your name does not need to be removed from that asset; therefore, probate of that asset is not required.

The third way of "avoiding" probate is through joint ownership of an asset, with the right of ownership transferred to the survivor. This method really does not "avoid" probate, but merely defers it until the passing of the surviving co-owner or joint tenant, as the case may be.

26. *Is probate ever beneficial?*

YES. There are situations in which probate can be the best strategy for the overall financial health of the estate. For example, if an estate has a heavy burden of nonsecured debt, probate will provide a window of opportunity for creditors of that estate to come forward and make a claim against it. If a creditor does not make a claim before that window closes, he/she will lose the ability to collect the outstanding debt.

Typically, though, probate is very costly. It's an expense that is unnecessary, nonbeneficial to the concerned parties, and inflicts needless pain and suffering.

27. *Is there a lot of paperwork to consider if I move or retire to a different state?*

NO. One of the best features of a properly drawn living trust is that it is portable. You can move it legally from state to state. Trusts are written to federal guidelines and therefore are valid nationwide. There are very few, if any, paperwork requirements when one moves a living trust into a different state. Rarely are even minor modifications needed from state to state. However, times change. It is wise to have your living trust reviewed in the new state of residence to make sure that these documents conform to public policy of that state.

28. *Will a separate tax return need to be filed when a revocable trust becomes irrevocable?*

YES. After the irrevocable trust is established, a federal trust income tax return, as may be required, is filed yearly under a 1041 trust tax return, using a trust ID number issued by the IRS. This number is obtained by filing an SS-4 request form with the IRS.

When using a revocable trust, the trustor(s) still files a 1040, as may be required, under his or her Social Security number(s). However, when an A-B living trust is employed, the passing of the first spouse will make one-half of that trust irrevocable and a 1041 trust tax return will have to be filed on the decedent's Trust B portion, using a trust ID number. The surviving spouse will still use his or her Social Security number and file a 1040 on the survivor's Trust A portion.

Upon the passing of the surviving spouse, the entire A-B living trust becomes irrevocable and a 1041 trust income tax return filed, as may be required. Subsequently, each year that the trust is in effect and has taxable income to it, a 1041 trust income tax return must be filed. This should cost no more to prepare than a standard 1040 return.

29. *Now that I know the benefits, can I have a high-quality living trust?*

YES. Please, don't put it off any longer. Contact an estate planner, financial or retirement planner, or an attorney *today*, one who offers a high-quality living trust, customized to your needs, at a reasonable price. Select one known for quality work, high level of service, knowledge, and with a good reputation. Beware of providers who do not specialize in the preparation of living trusts. Do your homework, ask around. Read other books and articles. Get educated in trusts and become an informed and knowledgeable consumer.

EMPOWER YOURSELF AND YOUR FAMILY!

Summary of the Disadvantages of Probate

1. *Fees and costs.* Attorneys' fees, executors' fees, and court costs can eat up to 10 percent of the *GROSS* amount of the estate.

2. *Delays.* Your beneficiaries might possibly have to wait up to two *YEARS* before actually receiving the estate.

3. *Loss of privacy.* Probate is a court-supervised process open to the general public. Anyone can find out about your personal and financial affairs.

4. *Inconvenience.* Your beneficiaries must work with attorneys, executors, and the court bureaucracy during the probate process to receive any income from the estate!

5. *Unintended upstart heirs.* An unhappy relative may have a lawyer challenge an estate to lock it up in probate court to extract a "piece of the action." During the battle, the rightful heirs may lose all or part of their inheritance.

Summary of the Advantages of a Living Trust

1. *Avoids probate.* All assets placed into a living trust pass to your beneficiaries without probate, avoiding all the problems involved with that process, including the costs, delays, loss of privacy, and inconvenience.

2. *Maintains family control during disability.* Your living trust provides for a successor trustee to manage your assets in case of disability during your lifetime.

3. *Saves estate taxes.* Where applicable, your living trust allows you to use straightforward, legal procedures to benefit from the savings on federal estate taxes.

4. *Avoids the joint tenancy tax trap.* There are serious dangers in holding title to assets as joint tenants. The property could become subject to creditor claims, left to unintended heirs, and be subject to unfavorable income taxes upon your death. A living trust avoids all of these problems.

THE POWER OF THE LIVING TRUST CAN BE YOURS.

One Final Thought

Life is a lot like the famous football game in which the score kept going back and forth between the two teams. Plays were run right up to the last second, when the final buzzer signaled the end of the game.

When the reporters asked the losing coach how it felt to lose such a close game, he replied, "We didn't lose that game. We simply ran out of time."

Unlike that coach, none of us can see how much time is left on the clock. We can keep score, but the final buzzer can sound at any time.

The living trust is on the winning team.

It's a winner's game plan.

Stephen C. Brecht's estate planning firm in Woodland Hills, California, will offer assistance and document packages to those desiring to set up a revocable living trust or other estate planning mechanisms. Direct your correspondence to Estate Planning Services, 22144 Clarendon Street, Suite 220, Woodland Hills, California 91367 or call (818) 888-1057.

[Note: Address subject to change].